# NEWS, IMPROVED
## HOW AMERICA'S NEWSROOMS ARE LEARNING TO CHANGE

Michele McLellan and Tim Porter

CQ PRESS

A Division of Congressional Quarterly Inc.
Washington, D.C.

CQ Press
1255 22nd Street, NW, Suite 400
Washington, DC 20037

Phone: 202-729-1900; toll-free, 1-866-4CQ-PRESS (1-866-427-7737)

Web: www.cqpress.com

Cover design: Matthew Simmons
Cover photos: shutterstock.com and veer.com
Composition: Auburn Associates, Inc.

⊚ The paper used in this publication exceeds the requirements of the American National Standard for Information Sciences—Permanence of Paper for Printed Library Materials, ANSI Z39.48-1992.

Printed and bound in the United States of America

11   10   09   08   07        1   2   3   4   5

**Library of Congress Cataloging-in-Publication Data**

McLellan, Michele.
    News, improved: how America's newsrooms are learning to change / Michele McLellan and Tim Porter.
        p. cm.
    Includes bibliographical references and index.
    ISBN-13: 978-0-87289-419-8 (alk. paper)
    ISBN-10: 0-87289-419-3 (alk paper)
    1. Journalism—Management.    2. Journalism—Study and teaching.    I. Porter, Tim
    II. Title.

PN4784.M34M35 2007
070.4068—dc22

                                                                    2007004874

# CONTENTS

*by Eric Newton*

*News, Improved* is for journalists who intend to thrive in the 21st century.

It is an exploration of the new world right in front of us, a manual for those ready to stop pining for the past and start growing with the future. The message: any journalist can learn to join the booming digital world of targeted, convenient, interactive media.

The digital revolution has, plain and simple, upended journalism. The speed at which information moves—and the new ways people consume it—are transforming what journalists need to know and do.

*News, Improved* describes how newsrooms can remake themselves. It highlights newspaper leaders who are taking charge of change. It visits newsrooms big and small that move as more creative teams of coordinated yet still independent thinkers. It tells of journalists who stay true to their best, most time-honored values as they innovate and become more open, closer even, to their audiences.

The key to all the above is strategic training.

This book sees hope even for daily newspapers, the media life form most endangered today. It focuses on them because they operate America's most important news collection system. Employing nearly half the country's 120,000 general news journalists, the dailies provide citizens with much of the news they use to run their governments and their lives. As Jack Knight wrote, good newspapers are what "bestir the people into an awareness of their own condition, provide inspiration for their thoughts and rouse them to pursue their true interests."

Some say such journalism is impossible in the digital age. At the Knight Foundation, we disagree. We think the future of news is everyone's to make or break.

The 21st century is bringing big changes to journalism. The one-way model of news—a journalist sends a message through a medium to an audience—is evolving. To survive, news people are reinventing each of the four elements in the model—the journalist, the message, the medium, the audience.

First, journalists are changing themselves. Newsrooms, once the refuge of quirky geniuses and raging individualists, now need people who can work well together. Newsroom culture can still be probing, exacting, compulsively curious and even quirky, but at the same time it must be open, diverse, tolerant and collaborative.

Second, journalists are changing the form and nature of their message. When interactive maps are better than police logs, they need to provide the maps. Journalists need to tap their own creativity, creating a steady stream of innovative products that put the news into greater, more meaningful context.

Third, journalists are changing their medium—to multimedia. Get the news once, then deliver it on the Web, the phone, the radio and the television as well as in the paper. The best journalists are finding ways to create tools and techniques to do it.

The fourth change: audiences. They are no longer simply viewers, readers or users. They are now news producers. Journalists need to find ways to engage and enlist their audiences in the fair, accurate contextual search for truth.

Journalist, message, medium, audience. Changing all at once seems too much. But it is being done in places like Hamilton, Ontario, and Bakersfield, California, and it can be done anywhere. The catch: doing things differently requires new and different skills. Transformation requires news organizations to find ways to spend more time, and even more money, on professional development. Today, it's more important for everyone to know what they are doing than it is to have one more staff member running around after one more story.

To demonstrate this, the Knight Foundation spent $10 million during the past four years on something we called the Newsroom Training Initiative.

*News, Improved* explains what our grantees accomplished. The Tomorrow's Workforce program convinced CEOs to let us work with willing newspaper editors to shape training programs that would move entire newsrooms. The Learning Newsroom demonstrated that more constructive newsrooms more readily adapt to changing times. NewsTrain showed how middle managers, the guardians of culture, can become advocates of good training when they get a little of it themselves. The Traveling Curriculum showed that newsrooms can raise standards and help each other meet them. News University showed that any journalist could get better just by going online.

The Newsroom Training Initiative reached, conservatively, 35,000 journalists. Our message, that training works, was convincing enough for newspaper companies belonging to the Southern Newspaper Publishers Association (SNPA) to donate $8 million to a permanent endowment to bring basic training to their employees in a program called the Traveling Campus. This was a major shift for an industry that invests a pitiful .4 percent of payroll in training (by the latest Inland Press Association estimates) while the average American business invests more than five times that amount.

SNPA has made a good start. The $100 billion a year news industry should not depend upon charity for training its own employees. But as the sun sets on our foundation's training initiative, we wonder: will the industry step up? So far, the answer is yes—and no. Our research shows that 3 in 10 news organizations are increasing training. New media and management training are high on the list of priorities. The glass is a third full.

If you are a good journalist, stuck at a news organization that doesn't seem to believe in its own future, what should you do? Leave? Yes, actually. If reasonable efforts—such as those described in this book—are not being tried, train yourself as best you can and go. The 20th century killed 1,000 daily newspaper newsrooms and 1,000 radio newsrooms. Media evolution doesn't favor the big or strong. It favors the nimble. Be nimble.

Profits are high enough to remake this industry. Web readership is soaring. Private companies are reinvesting. It's time for journalism training to grow up, from an ad hoc, budget-less, random act of kindness to a smart, professional way to help an entire newsroom get where it urgently needs to go.

We don't need another exposé of missed opportunities; we need to explore the opportunity that's right in front of us. That is the goal of *News, Improved*.

With good leaders, clear goals, an open culture and a specific plan, journalists can change any news organization, even a daily newspaper. The courageous tell us total change is just a few years away. We hope to see you there.

*Eric Newton is vice president of journalism programs at the Knight Foundation. He was founding managing editor of the Newseum; managing editor of the* Oakland Tribune; *editor of numerous books, including* Crusaders, Scoundrels, Journalists; Capture the Moment *and* News in a New America; *and a four-time Pulitzer Prize juror.*

## CHAPTER 1

# Closing the Leadership Gap

*Merely riding the current of change, complaining all the while, is a path that leads
only to cynicism and failure. It's seductively self-indulgent, but it's just plain
wrong. The alternative is choosing to act. That's leadership. And it's what these
times demand.*

—David Zeeck, executive editor, *Tacoma News Tribune,*
president, American Society of Newspaper Editors, 2006–2007

The reinvention of newspapers in the digital age requires the reinvention of
newsroom leadership.

Editors are discovering that the traditional, top-down "I-paid-my-dues-and-
now-it's-your-turn" style of management fails to foster the nimble thinking, collaboration and risk-taking newspapers need to overcome the changes in economics, demographics and technology that are transforming the news industry. They
are discovering they need to learn to change.

Newspaper print readership continues its decades-long decline. Good editors
know newspapers face deepening mediocrity and marketplace irrelevancy unless
they can figure out how to invent new forms of journalism and devise strategies
that will bring in readers and revenue.

But top editors also know, and admit privately, that they are ill equipped for the
task ahead. "Change or die" is an uncomfortable mantra for editors who have
spent their careers trying to build on the newsroom status quo. They have skills to
efficiently produce a newspaper but little experience in creating and leading
change in the way news is collected and distributed. In addition, researchers have
found newsrooms are among the most change-resistant workplaces.[1] Imagine the
difficulty: unprepared editors leading the unwilling into the unknown.

Even in the good newsrooms where we at Tomorrow's Workforce have spent the
past three years, there is a leadership gap. In the average newsroom, it is wide and
deep, the result of decades of neglect. When newspapers dominated local news
markets, enjoyed corpulent profits and doted on tradition, editors were promoted
because they were good at getting the most out of the existing system—not at
turning it upside down. They managed the controlled chaos of the newsroom, covering the beats, jumping on the big story and pulling off good investigations when

they could. These editors could write, edit and give directions without flinching, and do it under pressure for as long as the news demanded. First into the office, last out.

Many editors had neither the skill nor the desire to craft and execute a strategic plan (no need, we just cover the news), engage in two-way communication or delegate authority (no need, just do what I say). Despite occasional spurts of 20th-century news leadership, the average newspaper was run by a manager who did not have to worry about innovation or change.

"Every industry is both a beneficiary and a victim of its past," says Pierre Meyer, an industrial psychologist who has worked in newsrooms for more than 30 years.[2] "The history in newsrooms, even if you look back to the '60s and '70s, includes a lot of directive, in charge, I-know-what-we-should-be-doing leaders who moved up to executive editor. And they stayed with that for longer than they should have before people finally started to say, 'Wow, we've got to do something differently.'"

"Differently" means retooling newspapers, converting them from news factories into communication hubs that connect to their communities through multiple channels, digital and print. "Differently" means audiences that have thousands of news choices every day and can control how and when they get the news. "Differently" means journalists who can collect the news once and distribute it in many different ways and media. "Differently" means editors who can make plans, set goals, communicate and lead. And "differently" means training everyone to be able to take on a new role. Everyone, starting at the top.

In this chapter, we will show why leadership matters and why the times require a new set of leadership skills. We will tell the stories of editors and their journeys of change. We will examine actions and attitudes—many done unconsciously or out of habit—of editors that not only inhibit but actively discourage risk-taking in newsrooms. And we will look at the characteristics of good leadership and discuss how some newspaper editors have acquired them.

Reinventing leadership is not easy. Most people resist change, successful people the most strenuously. Why would a successful editor think that skills that worked so well in the past would not continue to do so in the future? As one high-ranking editor at a large newspaper told us during a visit to his newsroom, "I was a manager at the *Wall Street Journal.* I don't feel that I need training."

Other newsroom leaders, like Mike Jenner, executive editor of the innovation-minded *Bakersfield Californian,* embraced change. Change is part of his daily reality, Jenner says:

> My job has changed significantly in the last seven years. It's changed remarkably. The job I stepped into is a completely different job than the job I'm doing now. I used to do some editing, and now I do very little. . . . Much of what I do now is much less

focused on the day-to-day and the news itself and the newsroom itself, and a lot of it is focused outside in dealing with the public or other parts of the company, more strategic things than operational things—which I think is absolutely the way it should be. I've had to learn as I go.

## WHY LEADERSHIP MATTERS

The quality of a newspaper's leadership is directly connected to its ability to innovate. In its 2004 *New Readers* study of 50 large and small U.S. newspapers and 6,600 newspaper employees,[3] the Readership Institute at Northwestern University found that a newspaper with communicative, open leaders was more likely to have a newsroom staff that knew where the paper was going and how it intended to get there. That is important because engaged, energetic employees and clear strategic goals are key to constructive change.

Organizational culture expert Toni Antonellis says newspapers are learning the lessons of other companies that operate in highly competitive environments.[4]

If you're . . . getting your butt kicked on a regular basis, and competition is prolific, then you tend to be more mindful about what motivates people and what creates an environment of risk-taking and innovation and adaptability. Necessity is the mother of invention. I think that's true in a business context as much as it is in a personal context. We all grow when we're challenged. I'm not sure that up until the last five years we've been challenging our (newspaper) leaders to say, "How do we need to behave differently to change the dynamics of the organization?"

I can't tell you how many conversations I've participated in at the leadership level where they've said, "What are we going to do to change the organization?" versus saying "What are we going to do to change our behavior that will then create some change?"

There is plenty of help for editors who want to learn to change. Thousands of books are in print teaching leadership and management.[5] Leadership training is available. Organizations like The Poynter Institute for Media Studies and the American Press Institute offer rolling menus of seminars and workshops on leadership and management, as well as a plethora of columns, tips and other advice on being a better leader. The Poynter Web site alone contains 300 columns on leadership topics.[6]

Not surprisingly, newspaper leaders nimble and innovative enough to navigate the obstacle course of modern news media are beginning to emerge.

In 2003, for example, Dana Robbins, editor of *The Hamilton Spectator* in Ontario, Canada, responded to declining readership with what most newspapers consider a heretical makeover. Among other things, he killed off the business, entertainment and lifestyle sections, remade the sports section into a tabloid and used the money and staff time saved to launch a new magazine and an analysis section. The result:

> Two years later the *Spectator* has seen year-over-year growth in readership in the primary target audience of women as well as growth in readership overall. But that is not what pleases the editor the most. It is his newspaper's newfound capacity to be bold and try innovative things.[7]

Robbins has little patience for peers who continue to find reasons not to change their leadership practices. He recalls running into Antonellis at a Canadian newspaper conference. They wondered how newspaper editors, people who are up to the minute on current events, could be so far behind on the basics of management. As Robbins tells it:

"I said to her, 'How are you feeling?'

"She sort of shrugged.

"And I said, 'What?'

"She said, 'It's just that I've done this a thousand times.'

"We both sort of read each other's minds. I said to her, 'How appalling that 50 years after the rest of the world embraced things like understanding your audience, research, understanding the HR factor, understanding how culture impacts performance, yadda, yadda, yadda—you are actually in 2006 trying to convince the senior leadership of newsrooms that this stuff matters.'

"Honest to God! How is it possible in 2006 that we even have to try to convince people about things like culture? I'm trying to think of how the IBMs, the Apple computers, how if they were sitting in a conference of newspaper editors that they couldn't help saying when they walked out, 'What the hell! These people are dinosaurs!'"

Robbins tells a great story. But it is not the kind the newspaper industry wants told about itself—full of comical anecdotes about organizational buffoons who overstayed their welcome at the digital media party. If many newspaper editors had turned a deaf ear to Toni Antonellis' good advice about leadership, they heard well the cavalcade of bad news 2005 brought—more than 2,000 newspaper jobs eliminated, the meltdown of Knight Ridder (and its sale the follow-ing year) and Wall Street analysts' gloomy forecasts of more bad times to come. 2005 also was the year Rupert Murdoch chastised editors at the American Society of Newspapers Editors' convention for their complacency.

The flip side was that popularity of new media outlets soared. Google became a household name, an information service selling billions of dollars in advertising without a newsgathering staff and attracting more than 40 percent of all the news searches on the Web.[8]

In response, editors began to speak up about the need for innovation and how newspapers had to take control of their own future. Free newspapers, youth newspapers, ethnic media and digital products brightened a gloomy print media forecast. What had been debatable to many began to seem obvious. David Zeeck, whose Tacoma, Wash., newsroom participated in the Learning Newsroom project, says:

> Our choice couldn't be clearer. We can be swept along by a tide of change—a blizzard of technology, news as a commodity, multiplying competitors, the pressures of Wall Street and limited resources—or we can take who we are—experienced journalists, critical thinkers, people of integrity, skilled at asking good questions and analyzing data—and exert our energies and our talents to craft the best outcomes that we can imagine and deliver. Merely riding the current of change, complaining all the while, is a path that leads only to cynicism and failure. It's seductively self-indulgent, but it's just plain wrong.[9]

When Zeeck exhorts America's newspaper editors to "give readers leadership that produces more journalism worthy of the First Amendment" and "give our staffs leadership that demands excellence and demonstrates integrity" and "give our communities leadership that allows them a ringside seat to what we do and why we do it," he is pleading with his peers for change.[10]

## WHY LEADERSHIP IS CRITICAL TO NEWSROOM LEARNING

In 2002, the John S. and James L. Knight Foundation's study "Newsroom Training: Where's the Investment?" found the news industry lagged far behind comparable industries in providing professional development. Journalists said this lack of training was their No. 1 workplace complaint.[11]

In response, a coalition of more than 50 professional journalism groups called for an effort to encourage the news industry to invest more time and money in training. In 2003, Knight made $10 million in grants to create five training and research projects; the goal was to increase training nationwide to demonstrate that better training meant better journalism, and better journalism could increase the readership and usage of news outlets.

Northwestern University's Medill School won one of the grants in the Newsroom Training Initiative for our project, Tomorrow's Workforce. The project's goal was to convince participating newspapers that if they devoted more resources to training—and allocated them well—they would see measurable gains in news quality and audience appeal. The project's initial focus was on training for staff and midlevel editors, but as we began to visit newsrooms, leadership quickly emerged as an issue.

A key element of the project was a series of extensive interviews with staff, middle managers and newsroom executives at each newspaper. The interviews—more than 500 in total—explored perceptions of the newspaper's strengths and weaknesses, the quality of the management and the rank and file, and the amount and impact of available training.

In every newsroom, we found big differences of opinion between the top, middle and bottom layers. One of the nation's top metropolitan newspapers provides an example. The top tier of editors readily listed the newspaper's goals—more investigative reporting, more stories from the suburbs, more Page One enterprise and more stories told in nontraditional ways. But where the senior editors saw clarity, the staff saw confusion.

For one thing, the painstaking way important stories were edited made journalists less likely to want to do them. We wrote in our report:

> One reporter said finding out a story is going to Page One "ruins my day," because it promises intense and often contradictory scrutiny and direction. Editors and reporters alike said that "sequential editing" by senior editors is discouraging and reinforces the idea of mixed messages.

The editors were confounded. How could the staff be confused? Hadn't they told them again and again?

As we spent more time at the newspaper, we discovered there were five newsrooms within this one news organization—one focused on quality, another on quantity, one on visuals, another on investigations, yet another on the growing suburbs. And, while the newspaper's leadership thought it had articulated clearly the expectations and standards for each of these sub-newsrooms, no one had sorted out the considerable conflict and discomfort the multiple initiatives (or priorities) caused among the middle managers and staff charged with implementing them. This newsroom didn't only have a training issue; it also had a leadership issue.

During our newsroom interviews, we never had to fish for comments that exposed these sorts of yawning leadership gaps. Some samples include:

- "I do not have enough time for long-term planning and just grabbing someone for 10 minutes to see how things are going. I'm almost a creature of the daily news budget."—*Editor of a small newspaper*

- Each deputy managing editor "is so different from the next. They should spend more time together, know and respect each other. I feel they're competing against each other more than they need to."—*Midlevel editor at a metro*

- When, at a training session, the executive editor spoke, "I learned more from her there than I ever did in the newsroom. She needs to set a clearer vision." —*Midlevel editor at a metro*

- "There is a loud and clear message that the culture is changing, but we haven't seen that from the very top. . . . What's lacking is the clarion call."—*Reporter at a metro*

- "There is a sense that (the top two editors) want creativity, but it has to fit their taste. You never know if they're going to like it or not."—*Midlevel editor at a metro*

What we heard was a desire for more communication, cohesion, clarity and collaboration—all qualities of good leadership in the newspaper industry or any other.

## MANAGEMENT IS NOT LEADERSHIP: EDITORS BEHAVING BADLY

*The afternoon news meeting was already well under way when the assistant managing editor in charge of local reporting entered the conference room. He sat in a chair in the far back corner, passing up a seat at the big table filled with department heads and assistants in the middle of the room. The newspaper's editor stood up front, listening to the ritual recitation of news budgets. As a news day, this was not an exciting one, and the editor was having difficulty filling Page One.*

*Conversation drifted within a narrow range of topics—story length, art availability, the inevitable night meeting that might make Page One. As the meeting neared conclusion, with the A-1 list still holding several question marks, the assistant managing editor in the back of the room hadn't yet been heard from. A visitor, curious about the editor's lack of participation in the discussion, craned his neck to see why. In a glance, the reason for the AME's silence was evident: he was asleep.*

This true story of the sleeping editor suggests one difference between a good manager and a good leader. A good manager would wake the guy up. A good leader would address the unspoken issue in the room: Why, at this late hour, was the news report still in such flux? Why was the most important page in the newspaper so unplanned, so haphazardly thought through, so resolutely serendipitous that even with the evening deadline looming a roomful of experienced editors could not endorse with certainty, much less with passion, what its content would be?

In America's business schools, the distinction between management and leadership is fundamental. Even the blandly bureaucratic U.S. Small Business Administration devotes a page on its Web site to "Leading vs. Managing." For example, it distinguishes managers from leaders as the following:

Managers are very good at maintaining the status quo and adding stability and order to our culture. However, they may not be as good at instigating change and envisioning the future. On the other hand, leaders are very good at stirring people's emotions, raising their expectations, and taking them in new directions (both good and bad).[12]

Newsrooms need good managers. But more than ever, they need good leaders who are not "maintaining the status quo" because the status quo is costing newspapers readers, revenue and relevance.

Leadership, as Harvard Business School scholar and author John P. Kotter says, "produces movement." He elaborates:

> Throughout the ages, individuals who have been seen as leaders have created change, sometimes for the better and sometimes not. They have done so in a variety of ways, though their actions often seem to boil down to establishing where a group of people should go, getting them lined up in that direction and committed to movement, and then energizing them to overcome the inevitable obstacles they will encounter along the way.[13]

Top editors who have successfully changed their styles say senior editors must learn to let go of details and instead focus their time, energy and credibility on leading newsroom change.

Nick Pappas describes himself as an editor who had a reputation for "making the trains run on time." In his 30-year career, he was the kind of get-it-done, go-to guy who often flourishes in the newspaper business. But when he became editor in chief of *The Telegraph* in Nashua, N.H., his first job as top editor, he discovered his approach had to change from "all the kind of stuff that fits more under the M category of managing as opposed to the L category of leadership."

Says Pappas: "I see my job here being considerably different than it was before, where I was consumed by putting together the news budget every day. What do we have for Page One tomorrow? Not that, honestly, I don't care about that stuff. Obviously, I do, but I don't see that as one of my primary job responsibilities now. There is a considerable difference between managing and leading. One of the challenges I've had in the 11 months I've been in this job is making that distinction clear in my own head."

Keep in mind, there are times when leaders must be managers and get their hands dirty in the details. But mostly, they should lead. For example:

- Managers make the trains run on time. Leaders plan out the new track.

- Managers make sure beats are covered. Leaders help create new beats and new forms of coverage.

- Managers look inward, making sure the newsroom functions. Leaders look outward, continually repositioning the newspaper in an ever-changing world.

Leadership demands the flip side of a journalist's days as a hard-charging city editor or detail-obsessed reporter. Leaders are rewarded not for today's big-enterprise story but for their ability to think long-term, to express ideas clearly, to build working groups, to teach rather than do. Leaders embrace patience even at those maddening moments when they know, just absolutely know, that they could do it better themselves.

It is, says Robbins, *The Hamilton Spectator* editor, a matter of personal willpower.

> I find that discipline is required to be strategic and not tactical. It's excruciatingly difficult at times. Most of us came up through the ranks and it's easy to get drawn in. I like to tell that, oh, because there's this huge, sucking vacuum that pulls us back into the newsroom every day, but the reality is that's what I enjoy; that's what I like doing. It takes every fiber of my being when I walk by the city desk and hear them talking about a breaking story not to stop and insert myself into the conversation. I think that's a natural inclination. Most newsrooms are run by journalists. They're not run by professional leaders. It's not a skill set most of us have invested in at any point of our career.

Leaders, says psychologist and author Daniel Goleman, move the "collective emotions" of the organization toward a defined goal. According to Goleman:

> Leaders have always played a primordial emotional role. No doubt humankind's original leaders—whether tribal chieftains or shamanesses—earned their place in large part because their leadership was emotionally compelling. Throughout history and in cultures everywhere, the leader in any human group has been the one to whom others look for assurance and clarity when facing uncertainty or threat, or when there's a job to be done. The leader acts as the group's emotional guide. . . .
>
> In the modern organization . . . the leader has maximal power to sway everyone's emotions. If people's emotions are pushed toward the range of enthusiasm, performance can soar; if people are driven toward rancor and anxiety, they will be thrown off stride.[14]

## CLOSING THE LEADERSHIP GAP: WHAT NEWSPAPERS NEED NOW

The most successful newspaper editors in Tomorrow's Workforce and the Learning Newsroom, those who changed themselves and their newspapers, shared these traits:

- Belief that the status quo wasn't working.
- Willingness to let go of some authority and empower their staffs.
- Recognition that training improves their newsrooms.
- Tenacity to drive over the speed bumps of change.

Industrial psychologist Pierre Meyer describes how engaged leaders work the newsroom:

> They would be wandering around the newsroom chatting with people, asking them, "What are you doing? What's new? How can you handle that story differently?" They would literally be the catalyst for change. They aren't directing people, but they're guiding the thinking process and then encouraging people to try something out.

What does a newsroom leader need to learn to be able to do this? Consider this advice on the American Press Institute's Web site from Antoinette Taylor-Thomas, managing editor of the *Lancaster (Ohio) Eagle-Gazette:*

- "Trust your instincts, take risks and don't be afraid to voice your opinions or challenge the way things always have been done. The industry needs innovative thinkers more than anything now, and leaders can't be afraid to change or try new things."

- "Remember you need grooming and coaching along the way, so don't be afraid to ask for training, coaching and mentoring that will make you a stronger, well-rounded leader." [15]

Trust instinct. Take risks. Don't fear fear. Innovate. Grow yourself. That's a leadership development roadmap in 10 words.

For each editor, the path to personal reinvention must begin with self-assessment. A series of questions, answered honestly (and sometimes painfully), is the place to start:

- What are my strengths?
- What are my weaknesses?
- What are my values?
- What motivates me?
- What do I actually do every day?
- Should I be doing something else?
- What are my personal and professional goals?

Self-honesty can be unpleasant. None of us is perfect, and admitting that doesn't come easily for many people. But answering these questions is the start, your own personal training session. Here is how John Smalley, editor of the *La Crosse (Wis.) Tribune,* describes his transition:

> I had to be willing to look really honestly at my role in either helping or hindering the cause of training and the accomplishment of goals in the newsroom. It wasn't

always the most fun to dig into my own shortcomings, but it was very useful in the long run.

Through our conversations with editors like Smalley, two broad areas of leadership skills emerged as being critical to creating a dynamic, constructive newsroom. Today's newsroom leader must have:

- *Vision.* The leader must be able to imagine a long-term future for the newspaper within the context of its business conditions. She must be able to hold that creative vision in mind as the organization defines specific goals, crafts strategies to achieve them and encounters and overcomes obstacles.

- *Communication skills.* The leader must be able to communicate openly and clearly. A creative vision is useless unless the leader can connect the dots between the abstractions of long-term goals and necessities of the daily news product. He must be able to explain why change is necessary, to define which goals are most important and to guide the organization through the inevitable problems that will arise.

## A CREATIVE VISIONARY SEES THE POSSIBILITIES

Vision is a sense of place, an imagined destination, a continuously changing endpoint where a leader hopes to take the organization at some point in time, perhaps next year, maybe in five years, possibly a decade into the future.

Vision can be thought of as answers to two simple questions: Where would I like to go? When would I like to get there? Applied to a newspaper, these questions can be framed in newsroom terms: What would I like my news organization to look like or be capable of one year from today? How would the reporting differ? What would the structure of the newsroom look like? What new skills would my staff—or I—have?

Without a creative vision, a newsroom leader can never create positive, productive, intentional change. Yes, change is possible, but lacking vision, lacking a sense of direction and a desired outcome, the change is likely to be erratic, unintentional or contrary to purpose and even damaging to the quality of work being done.

Bob Zaltsberg, editor of *The Herald-Times* in Bloomington, Ind., a newspaper that participated in the Learning Newsroom project, said vision is "an easy word to throw around." To him vision refers to an editor's ability to keep his eyes focused on the future. "You need to see the possibilities," Zaltsberg said. "I don't think that I or anybody has a vision of exactly where it is we need to go, but I think that leaders in newsrooms today need to be able to envision some possibilities of what could work down the road."

John Kotter, the Harvard scholar, says a strong vision "simplifies hundreds or thousands of more detailed decisions . . . motivates people to take action in the right direction, even if the initial steps are personally painful (and) . . . helps coordinate the actions of different people, even thousands and thousands of individuals, in a remarkably fast and efficient way." [16]

Vision provides direction: "This is where we're going." Vision provides purpose: "This is why we're going there." Vision provides means: "This is how we're going to organize ourselves to do the things necessary to get there."

From vision, all other decisions flow. The newsroom leader must keep her vision for the newspaper in the forefront as she communicates with the staff. She must keep this focus as she allocates resources. She must keep her vision as she assesses the volatility of the conditions in her market. A vision is a strategic springboard for one possible future out of many. A newsroom leader must walk the balance beam between propagating that vision and amending it as conditions change. Hang on too long, and a vision becomes obsolete. Change too frequently, and it might never take hold.

In "Built to Last: Successful Habits of Visionary Companies," James C. Collins and Jerry I. Porras portray vision as a kind of life force:

> The essence of a visionary company comes in the translation of its own ideology and its own unique drive for progress into the very fabric of the organization—into goals, strategies, tactics, policies, processes, cultural practices, management behaviors, building layouts, pay systems, accounting systems, job design—into *everything* the company does. [17]

But vision, the authors say, is only the start. They relate the Parable of the Black Belt, the tale of a young martial arts student and his sensei. It starts with the student, having completed his training, kneeling before his sensei to get his black belt. But the sensei says he must pass one more test.

"I am ready, responds the student, expecting perhaps one final round of questioning.

"You must answer the essential question: What is the true meaning of the black belt?"

"The end of my journey," says the student. "A well-deserved reward for all my hard work."

The sensei waits for more. Clearly, he is not satisfied. Finally, the sensei speaks. "You are not yet ready for the black belt. Return in one year."

A year later, the student kneels again in front of the sensei.

"What is the true meaning of the black belt?" asks the sensei.

"A symbol of distinction and highest achievement in our art," says the student.

The sensei says nothing for many minutes, waiting. Clearly, he is not satisfied. Finally, he speaks. "You are still not ready for the black belt. Return in one year."

A year later, the student kneels once again in front of the sensei. Once again, the sensei asks: "What is the true meaning of the black belt?"

"The black belt represents the beginning—the start of a never-ending journey of discipline, work, and the pursuit of an ever-higher standard," says the student.

"Yes. You are now ready to receive the black belt and begin your work."[18]

## CLEAR COMMUNICATION TRANSLATES THE VISION INTO ACTION

*All leadership takes place through the communication of ideas to the minds of others.*[19]
—Charles Cooley, sociologist

Communicating is more than telling people what to do. A visionary newsroom leader who cannot get his message across will never be able to effect change. One of our Tomorrow's Workforce papers provides a good illustration. At this newspaper—a midsize operation in a semirural town—the managing editor sat in her office, frustrated.

Several times she mentioned one department head. He's a good editor, she said, but he can't delegate. He back-edits the work of his assistant. He rewrites without telling the reporters. He works the longest hours on the paper, but never puts any effort into improving the work of his reporters or line editors. The result: a copy flow bottleneck, resentment by reporters and other editors, and frustrated senior editors.

The managing editor had mentioned this many times. "I must have told him 20 times," she blurted out. "I don't know why he can't learn."

This is a classic example of telling, not teaching (here's what you need to do versus here's how you can learn how to do that) and of talking and not communicating (the former is all about you; the latter is all about the other person). This editor knew how she wanted the midlevel editor to change, but she didn't have the communication skills to guide him along that path.

Newsroom learning cannot take place without ongoing, almost relentless communication by newsroom leaders. Julia D. Wallace, editor of *The Atlanta Journal-Constitution*, says the biggest lesson she learned from the ambitious strategic training program she launched in 2004 was "the importance of over-communicating." Find as many ways as you can, she advises, to say and to show "This is where we're going. This is where we're going."

Dropping certain practices, even temporarily, that tend to undermine the main message is another way of reinforcing the vision:

- An editor who wants to encourage greater decision making by the staff might stop asking to see a fax of the front page every night before it goes to press.

- An editor who wants to encourage creative risk might change her daily critique from one that red-inks design and reporting flaws to one that looks at whether the print and on-line reports reflect creativity.

- An editor who prefers to spend most of his day locked in his office might work the room regularly, as Meyer suggests.

- An editor who champions enterprise journalism might refrain from chastising editors about missed stories at the daily meeting.

- An editor who exhorts staff to get more stories about people in the newspaper might make sure those stories get good play rather than saving big newsroom kudos for long investigative pieces.

Leadership communication has a simple purpose: clarifying direction and moving people in that direction. Newsroom leaders who are serious about involving nonmasthead managers and other staff in creating strategic change must ask them what they think the newspaper's priorities should be, what type of training they need to make those priorities a reality and how they think the newsroom should be set up to get it all done. Eventually, after these managers and staff realize they won't be dispatched to the night cop beat for speaking plainly, they will say what they think—whether you like it or not.

Even with constant, clear communication the path to change will not always be a smooth one.

EXPECT TO HEAR FRUSTRATION

Progress will come slowly at first. People will react to change initiatives out of self-interest. Senior editors may use any sign of a setback to push for a change in direction. Midlevel managers may use a lack of momentum to dig in and return to past practices. Reporters and photographers may cite lack of immediate change as the failure of yet another flavor-of-the-day management fling. Top editors will experience midnight-at-the-refrigerator desires to quell these frustrations with a binge of nostalgia: It was easier before! (Maybe) It was better before! (No) It's never going to end! (Yes).

EXPECT TO SMOOTH RUFFLED EGOS

Creation of a shared strategic plan, even among the senior management team (much less the newsroom staff as a whole), requires that egos be kept leashed. Remember, when you ask people what they think, they'll tell you—and then they'll expect someone to do something about it. Are you comfortable with sharing power, with enabling rather than making decisions, with creating a community of leaders throughout your newsroom?

### Expect to Clarify Confusion

No one knows the future of newspapers. Standing still is no longer a survival option; the only roadmap to the future is a vague one. Newsroom leaders of the future must be comfortable with discomfort, and they will need to adjust course. In the digital world, goal posts really do move.

### Expect to Forgive Mistakes

The obsession with avoiding mistakes is one of the prime characteristics in the organizational culture of newsrooms. The key word here is obsession. Catching errors is good. Paying so much attention to catching errors that it paralyzes your organization is bad. Explaining the difference is key.

## GROWING TOMORROW'S LEADERS FROM TODAY'S EDITORS

Increasing numbers of editors are finding different forms of leadership that allow their newsrooms to commit daily journalism in new, more innovative, more empowering ways.

"People are beginning to say, 'Hmmm, we've got to do something differently,'" says Meyer. "And I would even say that those voices have increased and the volume has gotten a lot louder in the last three years."

Dana Robbins, at *The Hamilton Spectator,* agrees. He sees a renewed energy within the newspaper industry and its leadership ranks. "I think we really are on the cusp of a renaissance," he says. "I am absolutely convinced of that. Not that we're not in for difficult times in the future and we're not going to maybe go through some seismic changes—most definitely we will. When I think back to when, for example, I was a young city editor, or even longer ago when I was a reporter, there was a sleepiness about this industry. It was not necessarily a place you thought of as terribly dynamic with really sharp intellect, a place that was sort of changing and grappling with new concepts and new paradigms. Now, it feels very much like that."

As an example, Robbins mentions the Readership Exchange, an informal "group of editors from across Canada and the States who are buzzed about readership." He sat in on a recent meeting. "These are young bright minds who could, quite honestly, be working in any industry," he says. "They are sharp, bright intellects who are really engaged in terms of understanding the audience and how they can reach it and how they can do a better job capturing their attention. When I contrast that with 15, 20 years ago, I am really quite struck that there's so much more intellectual depth in our industry now than there was."

In the end, becoming a news organization leader instead of a newsroom manager is really about personal courage. That's what it takes to look honestly at oneself, to discard skills that have made your career, to learn and rely on new skills, to set a path for the future and lead a group forward.

Look at John Smalley, editor of the *La Crosse Tribune*. "At the risk of overstating this and being a little on the melodramatic side," he says, "I really do feel like I had a bit of an epiphany."

Smalley had worked his way up the food chain to the top spot. He describes life on the copy desk: "The whole gig is 'give me copy, give me copy, give me copy. I need to fill up these pages. Just keep it coming and keep it coming, and I'll tell you when to stop.' It was all about the production mentality. By necessity. That's how you survived—by being able to produce a local section every night." When he became editor at *La Crosse*, he fashioned his leadership style around "that production, feed-the-beast mentality."

"I always felt good when we had lots and lots of bylines," he says. "I was also a big byline counter. I felt the need to do that."

Smalley worked with consultant Judy Pace Christie of Tomorrow's Workforce. They discussed his strengths and weaknesses. He realized he could not "unknowingly or subtly, send this message that, 'It's all about production' and, at the same time, talk about how we want to be a quality newspaper and we're committed to training." He stopped counting bylines. The paper continued to be filled every day. But the stories were better. "That was one of the things I kind of had to come to terms with," he said, "It's OK that the budget isn't always as deep and as long as you think it maybe should be, or as you've been accustomed to wanting . . . if what's on the budget is the right stuff, if what's on the budget is better stuff than it used to be."

## PERSONAL LEADERSHIP TRAINING: GETTING IN SHAPE FOR CHANGE

There is no magic change bullet for leadership. But willingness to change is the first step. Then self-assessment and reflection. As Smalley said: "I had to be willing to look really honestly at my role in either helping or hindering the cause of training, and the accomplishment of goals in the newsroom. It wasn't always the most fun to dig into my own shortcomings, but it was very useful in the long run."

It may be difficult for top editors to identify strengths and weaknesses on their own, and they won't necessarily get candid feedback from their staffs.

To get a fuller picture, consultants like Antonellis and Meyer recommend that top executives receive confidential "360-degree" reviews, evaluations of their performance by superiors, peers and subordinates. These three-dimensional evaluations can be done through in-house training modules or with outside consultants.

"Getting somebody to be accurately self-aware might necessitate getting candid feedback from their staff, not just from their peers or from their boss, because top executives often model their bosses, and colleagues might exhibit similar behaviors," says Antonellis. "There is a behavioral history in any organization. If you're trying to change leadership behaviors or patterns it's important to zero base your assumptions about what great leadership looks like today."

At the same time, Antonellis cautions: "Incorporating the practice of 360 reviews can be enormously helpful but should be approached with great care. There needs to be an agreement about the skills and behaviors (competencies) that will drive performance and inspire a culture of innovation, adaptability and risk-taking. Finally, leaders need to be open to feedback. I think it's important to note that this isn't about identifying what's 'bad'; it's about recognizing what has to evolve."

Melanie Sill, executive editor of *The News & Observer* in Raleigh, N.C., a Tomorrow's Workforce newspaper, used 360 reviews. "It required me and the other newsroom leaders to consider our own needs to improve and grow, as well as training needs of the rest of the staff," she says.

Sill also attended a weeklong Center for Creative Leadership program to learn how to coach, how to hear feedback from others and how to resolve conflicts. "I wish I'd done it 10 years ago."

*The Oregonian* in Portland also used 360 reviews for its top editors and team leaders. One team leader described the training as "incredibly powerful. It did help me. It helped my boss. . . . It isolated those things I needed to work on, and I started working on them."

Learning to lead can be as uncomplicated as reading good books, such as *"A Force for Change"*[20] or *"Primal Leadership,"*[21] and talking openly about leadership skills in the newsroom. It could mean using the services of training institutions like The Poynter Institute and the American Press Institute. Or, as Sill did, turning to groups outside the news community, like the Center for Creative Leadership.

The important thing is not to go it alone. "Find a coach," says Meyer, "not necessarily an outside, professional coach. Maybe it's somebody inside. Maybe it's a trusted or older individual who's been around a long, long time and who knows the organization and has got the guts to say, 'Hey, that didn't work very well.'"

Once you've gotten feedback on your performance, made your plan and changed, what's the final step? It is willingness to keep learning and changing.

Transforming newspaper newsrooms requires a great amount of organizational willpower and individual self-discipline. The leadership must be able to see beyond the daily, weekly and seasonal news cycle, which is built around delivering a finished product within preset timeframes. Modern news media are dynamic and ever-changing. The institutions and individuals who work in them must be the same, constantly asking, "What do we want to be?"

## CHAPTER 2

# Goals: Knowing Just Where You're Going

*A vision "is only one of thousands of steps in a never-ending process of expressing the fundamental characteristics we identified (in) visionary companies."*
—James Collins and Jerry Porras, "Built to Last"

**O**nce a newspaper knows where it wants to go, has a vision, its training work has really only just begun. Now the ideal must become real, evident by changes in the content of the news product, the behavior of the journalists and the newsroom's relationship with its audience. Between vision and result lie strategic goals. Vision is a destination; goals are the road map.

Reinventing a newspaper can take years. Goals make it easier for editors to lead during that time. They demystify an uncertain future. They give a newsroom a sense of progress, even comfort. "Most staffers are not afraid to change once they understand the goals," says Julia D. Wallace, editor of *The Atlanta Journal-Constitution.*

Unlike most other businesses that create things for consumers, many newsrooms don't engage in strategic planning. A strategic plan defines specific goals for new products, developing processes (including training) to create the products, setting a time frame for achieving those goals and having a method to measure success.

Clear goals are the workaday expression of the leadership vision and the second element of a strategic development program that can transform a newspaper from a static, reactive organization into a dynamic, purposeful one.

At the *Journal-Constitution,* a set of goals formed the foundation of an ambitious— and successful—strategic training initiative. "We talked about those goals all year," says Wallace. "We rewarded good work in these areas in our best-of-quarter awards. We discussed them at news meetings. We pointed to them in kudo notes. Our training sessions were built around" them. The result was "real movement" in the newspaper—more watchdog reporting, more ways of telling stories and more positive response from readers.

In this chapter we will look at ways newspapers can turn vision into definable goals. We will discuss the need to set priorities that everyone can understand. We also will examine the importance of continual communication about goals. And we will tell the story of how one newspaper accomplished a lot more when it stopped trying to do everything at once.

When we asked top editors at the Tomorrow's Workforce newspapers about the vision for their newspapers, many referred us to their mission statements, often pretty vague stuff. Many mentioned "improving writing," "better beat coverage" or "expanding diversity." Few had specific plans about how to get to where they really wanted to be.

Is a mission statement a goal? Not really. Yet when we asked for goals, our editors would turn to their computers, hunt for a file of the statement, hit the print key and hand us a copy. Or they would find it in the employee handbook. One kept it on the newsroom wall. True, a good mission statement can provide the newsroom with a sense of journalistic purpose; but it is rarely a real vision crafted to address the unique conditions of that individual newspaper's market. And it is never a set of concrete organizational goals that will move the newspaper from Point A to Point B.

From newspaper to newspaper, the mission statements sounded similar. Some examples:

- "The (newspaper) strives to be the best regional newspaper in the United States. Our daily mandate is to be essential, authoritative and engaging."

- "The newsroom's mission is to provide relevant, timely and useful news and information that will help people make intelligent, informed choices, both large and small, in their daily lives and as they take part in the democratic process."

- "The staff of (the newspaper) believes in the indispensable role of journalism to inform, engage and empower readers."

- "Our mission in the newsroom is to provide a complete, accurate and appealing news report to our audience each day. We thrive on local but seek to provide a useful state, nation and world report as well. We seek to engage our readers, to inform and to entertain them."

To be the best, to be essential, to provide relevant and timely news, to engage and empower, to inform and entertain—we certainly can't argue with any of these desires. But they don't provide a vision of a newspaper's future in the highly competitive and ever-changing marketplace for news and information. In the end, a mission statement is a hollow substitute for the articulated vision and well-defined goals that comprise a real strategy.

Peter M. Senge, the developer of the concept of the "learning organization," tells this anecdote about vision statements in his book "The Fifth Discipline":

Recently, one of my . . . colleagues was explaining to two managers how our group works with vision. Before he could get far, one of the managers interrupted.

"We've done that," he said. "We've written our vision statement."

"That's very interesting," my colleague responded. "What did you come up with?"

The one manager turned to the other and asked, "Joe, where is that vision statement anyhow?"

Writing a vision statement can be a first step in building shared vision, but, alone, it rarely makes a vision "come alive" within an organization.[1]

In other words, a vision is not really a shared destination unless you can explain it without looking for the piece of paper.

It is easy to see how a defining vision leads to questions about goals and standards. If a newspaper today wants to be, for example, "essential" or "engaging," it must ask questions about audience, subject matter, platform and even price. (Can something be essential if it is free?) Editors must ask: Who should read our newspaper? What are we going to put in it (content) and in which form (narrative, visual, interactive)? Which form (print or Web) will make our content most "essential"? This line of questioning examines a newspaper's strengths and weaknesses and can lead to concrete plans for change. In this case, the answer to "how to be more engaging" might be to use a wider variety of story forms, a goal several Tomorrow's Workforce newspapers adopted based on Readership Institute research.

Toni Antonellis, a leadership and organizational culture expert who works with newspapers, says the single best thing newsroom leaders can do is to be very specific about what success looks like.

We shy away from hard metrics in newsrooms, creating an environment of confusion. People can't really achieve performance targets through mission or vision statements. The same is true for loosely defined business goals. Saying you want to increase readership may or may not move the needle. But if you say our primary goal is to increase female readers—ages 35 to 55—by 5 percent in the next 18 months, people can be very deliberate implementing a strategy to hit that goal. They know what success looks like and where to focus their energy. Adding dimensions to targeted goals by defining audience targets and answering what eyeballs you want to own in print, digital niches furthers your chances for success.

The second most valuable thing leaders can do is to articulate the assumptions around which strategies have been built. Our world has changed. The way we compete, serve our readers and advertisers has changed. People need to know the new rules for engagement.

Antonellis' specifics are necessary for a newsroom to break down a broad vision statement into well-defined goals that newsroom leaders can easily explain.

Bob Zaltsberg, editor of the *Herald-Times* in Bloomington, Ind., worked with Antonellis as part of the Learning Newsroom project. He says the journey from vision to goals demands continual attention and communication from top editors. "It's a lot harder to implement than it is just to talk about," he says. "What you really have to do is go one step at a time. You have to show people what the next step is going to be on the way to whatever the vision is."

Zaltsberg envisions the *Herald-Times* becoming a newspaper that is a conduit for content created by readers—photographs, personal essays and other forms of do-it-yourself journalism. To demonstrate that it could be done, the staff created a section devoted to local pets. Frivolous? No, because it proved the larger point that the staff could "engage a group of readers and get them to contribute information that we think people are interested in reading in print or online."

Guiding editors to define and prioritize newsroom goals was key to the Tomorrow's Workforce success stories. The newspaper editors we worked with had given much thought to where they wanted their newspapers to go, but most had not translated those destinations into the segmented steps that would take them there—do this first, then this, later that.

In chapter 1 we discussed how our process of newsroom discovery—interviews about strengths, weaknesses, communication and training—quickly expanded to include leadership. Just as quickly, we added goals. What were they? Which were most important? How were they perceived at different levels of the newsroom? Later, when we reported to top editors on the state of their newsrooms, many told us the answers to these questions were eye-opening.

"I found (the) feedback to be among the most helpful advice I've ever received," said John Smalley, editor of the *La Crosse (Wis.) Tribune*. "(It) was fair and encouraging, but also very honest and clearly identified some issues I needed to deal with, which has been enormously useful to me."

Identifying goals. Communicating them. Breaking them down into daily work. These are the types of "thousands of steps" of visionary companies described by authors James Collins and Jerry Porras. Yes, thousands of steps. Continual learning. Perpetual growth. Constant movement. It is a discipline of self-improvement that becomes business as usual. For a newspaper, it means becoming an organization that is continually self-assessing, learning and adapting in order to take control of its own future.

"The critical question asked by a visionary company," say Collins and Porras, "is not 'How well are we doing?' or 'How can we do well?' or 'How well do we have to perform in order to meet the competition?' For these companies, the critical question is 'How can we do better tomorrow than we did today?'"[2]

Now, there's a mission.

## GOAL NO. 1: DECIDE YOU REALLY NEED GOALS

There is a scene in "Alice in Wonderland" often used to illustrate the need for goals. Alice, arriving at a fork in the road, asks the Cheshire Cat for advice:

"Would you tell me, please, which way I ought to go from here?"

"That depends a good deal on where you want to get to," said the Cat.

"I don't much care where—" said Alice.

"Then it doesn't matter which way you go," said the Cat.

"—so long as I get somewhere," Alice added as an explanation.

"Oh, you're sure to do that," said the Cat, "if you only walk long enough."

Training without goals is like driving without directions—eventually, like Alice, you will arrive *somewhere*, but it may not be where you want to go.

Ill-defined goals are a big contributor to the "us versus them" culture in newspaper newsrooms. (See chapter 3, "Newsroom Culture: No More Whining.") In some newspapers, goals are either nonexistent ("hey, we can't plan for news") or so vague ("better writing") as to offer infinite interpretation. Or they are so numerous that you can play a daily game of ping-pong goals, bouncing from one priority to the next, in ways that may in fact compete or even conflict. Or—the most common problem—top editors can recite the goals but staff cannot.

Many frontline journalists viewed goals (when they knew them) with skeptical disregard. To them the goals were empty slogans—annual embroidery from the front office, unsupported by budget, training, attitude or action. "We have a lot of these goals," one reporter said. "They seem to change every quarter." This view is, of course, self-perpetuating: "They say what they want, but we never change."

Only daily communication—or, as editor Zaltsberg says, "through conversation after conversation after conversation"—can undo those kinds of daily messages. And clear goals make daily communication much easier.

## GOALS DON'T HAPPEN BY ACCIDENT

A high-ranking editor of one the country's top 20 newspapers mentioned to us that his newspaper's front page is "often a happy accident." In other words, what the half-million readers of this newspaper saw was the result of an editorial process that was opportunistic and more the luck of the daily draw than the product of a long-term strategy.

That is the crux of old-school thinking. Some things go right, some go wrong, news happens and there you are at the end of the day: the happy accident of Page One. This works fine if you have a staff of a thousand, but what if you aren't so lucky?

The opposite of accidental journalism is intentional journalism. This approach is based on creating editorial goals that are supported by resources and training with the *intent* of serving a specific audience. It is journalism with a purpose, combining the needs of readers with the values of journalists.

John Pea, editor of the *Gaston Gazette*, a Tomorrow's Workforce newspaper in Gastonia, N.C., tried intentional journalism when planning coverage of the 2004 presidential election. Says Pea:

Instead of trying to look the same as practically every other newspaper the day after, we tried an experiment. Our front contained every possible race and ballot question of interest to our community, but in the form of one- or two-graph items, the numbers in tables and the pictures of winners. No giant pictures of Bush and Kerry with 300-point hammerheads.

The feedback we got from readers was overwhelmingly positive. One local doctor, who chased after me in a parking lot, made a point to emphasize how great he thought it was to be able to get all that information in one place quickly.

By the way, press association and other industry judges weren't so kind. "Too busy" were the words of one judge.[3]

One of Pea's goals for the *Gazette* was to be unique, to separate his newspaper from the competition. To do so he and his staff engaged in a series of innovative remakes of the *Gazette*'s front page, including several that used a spadea—a wrap around the front page—to summarize the day's news. Readers wanted the summary but hated the spadea.

"The plan now involved turning 1A into a refer front," says Pea. "But with a twist. We would have a 'cover' story in the top half of the page. It had to be local, or a localized version of a wire story.

"One other requirement of the big story was a summation of why this story should be important to the reader. 'What about here?' 'What's the deal?' 'What does this mean?' 'Why should you care?' Those are examples of the questions we pose daily and, hopefully, answer.

"New prototype printed. New set of focus groups. The result: They didn't just like it . . . they loved it."[4]

The *Gazette* connected the steps of a strategic development program—goals, learning and assessment. It wanted to be unique and to be local. It learned to innovate and take risks. It got feedback on its efforts. It put more weight on the opinions of readers and less on those of peer journalists. The result was a Page One that was intentional, not accidental.

This may seem basic. But after decades of this kind of talk and these sorts of examples, the average newspaper still has a long way to go. Despite trends like "newsrooms without walls" in the 1980s and "civic journalism" in the 1990s, the newsgathering process at many newspapers is still a template built on beat systems born in the age of the newspaper of record. This generic news template does not reflect the needs, desires and idiosyncrasies of specific communities. Content analyses of the newspapers participating in Tomorrow's Workforce showed that about two-thirds of all stories in the main news, local news and business sections were the same old formulaic reports on government agencies, the institutional news that is easy for papers to grind out but hard for readers to digest.

The "hey, it's news" approach served newspapers well when print sat atop a fixed news hierarchy more than 40 years ago. In every decade since, news media have become increasingly more complex, a change that accelerated in the 1990s with the rise of the Internet. The popularization of social networking, personal publishing and other Web 2.0 tools in the first decade of the 21st century created a truly interactive, multidimensional media environment. This dynamic, digital world doesn't put much value on yesterday's news, newspapers' main stock in trade.

The question a newspaper must confront is this: Is the hard-wired newsroom structure out of date? Is such a passive, serendipitous approach to newsgathering still sufficient in today's society? Can editors keep waiting for the "happy accident"? We believe they can't.

Remember the snoozing editor from chapter 1, the fellow who dozed off during the afternoon news meeting? He begs the question: When editors are not excited about their own front pages, how can they expect the readers to be?

At the *News & Record* in Greensboro, N.C., editor John Robinson decided the answer was to develop content unique to his community. He dropped some expensive wire services so the newspaper could use the money for more local reporting, including publishing blogs by reporters and editors before such Web sites became popular. Robinson's blog, The Editor's Log, lays out the paper's annual goals: even more local news, more emotional journalism, more contributions from readers and more digital news products. He shares his goals with readers:

- "Our goal in 2006 is to give you even more news and information that you cannot get elsewhere. We won't neglect national and international news, but the days in which wire services dominate the front page are waning at mid-size newspapers across the country."[5]

- "We will write more stories that impact your lives. The best journalism touches a nerve, either because it reveals an injustice, speaks to your heart or causes you to act."

- "Stories, columns and photos by readers will get greater visibility. We know that our readers know more than we do about a good number of subjects. We want to tap that knowledge and encourage you to write what you know for the benefit of the community."

- "We will expand the ways you can get news and information from us, and the ways you can talk with us and each other. Expect more blogs, forums, multimedia programs, pod casts, photo galleries and videos."

These are the kinds of clear goals that help newspapers change.

Some newspapers are forced to reorganize. Others want to. Either way, the questions editors ask themselves are the same: If I could use the same people and money to create any news operation I wanted, in today's digital world, what would I do? Would I create the same beats, the same departments, the same production and decision-making processes? Would I fill the newsroom seats with the same people who are there now? Would I design the paper and its Web site in the same formats? And the answer, almost always, is "of course not."

A vision, goals and training are all elements of getting from where a newsroom is today to the one that will survive the multimedia 21st century.

The Committee for Concerned Journalists (CCJ), a staff development project associated with the Project for Excellence in Journalism, worked with more than 120 newspapers over five years on core journalistic skills and values training. It found a clear connection between the clarity of goals and the success of training. In post-workshop surveys of their client newsrooms, the CCJ found:

> Those newsrooms that were most successful in implementing changes and suggestions were generally those where the manager had a clear sense of what he/she wanted the training to accomplish before the visit. Workshops were especially effective when managers primed their staffs to focus on particular goal areas in the training and think about how to incorporate them into daily routines.

Intentional journalism is the product of clear goals and purposeful training. Even the fastest-breaking news can be covered by journalists capable of reporting and thinking at the same time. Quality doesn't have to be a lucky fluke of accidental journalism.

## URGENCY AND PRIORITIES: WHAT'S IMPORTANT NOW?

*Only three? You're kidding.*
> —*Atlanta Journal-Constitution* editor responding to announcement of
> the newspaper's annual training priorities

*Ten things are not priorities. Ten things are a list.*
> —Becky Gregory, managing editor, *Waco Tribune-Herald*

Newsrooms that have goals, at least the ones we worked in, typically have too many of them. When there are more than a few, they aren't goals anymore; they become a giant to-do-list that never gets done because no one knows where to start.

Tomorrow's Workforce editors faced a glut of priorities. Sometimes, it had piled up over years. Few had winnowed it by asking, "What's important now?" An editor at a small newspaper said "a lack of focus and priorities" was holding it back. "By having no priorities," he said, "everyone is in a constant state of busyness, leaving no time for reflection or planning or good decision making."

To help newspapers develop strategic learning plans, we found we first needed to help senior editors and staff members set the goals and priorities of their newspapers. What usually emerged from these sessions was a list of lengthy, complex and often conflicting initiatives.

Two examples follow.

### Newspaper No. 1

The editors of this paper at first had difficulty identifying priorities, but by the time we met with them a second time had compiled a substantial list, including:

- Developing an ethics policy

- Putting more resources into local neighbors sections

- Doing personnel evaluations

- Having all newsroom employees receive customer service training

- Starting a weekly brown-bag training session led by department heads

- Planning better

- Improving the Web site

- Implementing an ongoing redesign

- Reinvigorating features content

### Newspaper No. 2

Senior editors at this paper had no problem articulating the newsroom's many initiatives. They did not, however, agree about which were the most important:

- Developing content to attract younger readers

- Winning a heated news war with a competitor in a growing suburb

- Enhancing multimedia capability and output

- Increasing quantity and quality of enterprise

- Producing better Sunday and investigative stories

- Generating enough community news to fill dozens of weekly sections

- Increasing the overall level of general excellence

- Making the paper and its content more diverse

- Raising the skill level of line editors

It is possible to do all of the things on these lists. But we don't recommend that approach.

A vision helps organize goals, helps determine which are the best and which need to get done first. That type of thinking focuses a newsroom's efforts and lines up the resources needed to get the goals accomplished. The laundry list approach dilutes the effort, lowers the chances of success and tends to leave half-finished goals that drag on from year to year.

Goals have a shelf life. What's important now may not matter next year. And some goals cannot be accomplished without doing something else first. For example, the staff is young. They need interviewing and source development training, as well as computer-assisted reporting skills. Which comes first? We'd say the basics. Two other examples:

- A newspaper wants to give midlevel managers and staff more say in strategic decision making. But the senior editors are autocratic and poor communicators. Which is more important: Forming staff committees, or immersing the senior editors in leadership training? Nothing can happen with truculent managers. We'd say you should deal with them first.

- A newspaper wants more narrative writing from its reporters, but line editors don't have the skills to edit this type of work. Which is more important: training the reporters or training the editors? Trick question. We'd do both together; the goals are codependent.

Moving money and people tells the staff what is a priority. An editor who sees that the Web is critical to the newspaper's future will systematically begin to shift a significant amount of resources from print to online. That editor finds a way to train people to take advantage of digital journalism tools. She says things like, "This is the year of the Web." The signal is clear.

In Atlanta, the *Journal-Constitution* put online editors and producers in each newsroom department. Editors in the conference room looked at a screen with the Web site and discussed the most popular stories. "We've spent three, four, five years talking about online," says Julia Wallace, the *Journal-Constitution*'s editor, "making it much more a part of the conversation, and some of the physical things we've done have had the most impact. . . . What you do physically changes the conversation. The whole thing is what you do, not what you say."

## ONE NEWSPAPER'S STORY: FROM TWO DOZEN PRIORITIES TO THREE PILLARS

The *Journal-Constitution* is one of the nation's biggest and best newspapers. It also has a long-held commitment to training, one signified by the presence of a training editor on its staff.

In 2003, its newsroom provided an average of nine hours of training per employee, higher than most newspapers in the industry. Newsroom executives had begun teaching classes to more than 100 midlevel editors. Senior editors were exploring ways to improve performance evaluations for all staff members. And a four-day-a-week newsroom-training director replaced one previously shared half-time with Cox Newspapers corporate.

But Wallace, promoted to *Journal-Constitution* editor just a year earlier, thought the newspaper could do a much bigger, better job. She was right.

The *Journal-Constitution* developed a focused set of editorial priorities and used them to build an aggressive in-house training program that produced dramatic change in the newspaper. The core elements of this effort—goal-setting, staff engagement and management participation—can serve as a model for any newspaper regardless of size.

When we first visited the *Journal-Constitution* newsroom in mid-2004, signs of a major transition were evident. Many of the paper's more than 450 staff members were enthusiastic about the creative direction of the new leadership but unsure of what it meant to their work. The newsroom had a long tradition of quality journalism. Employees were proud to work at the *Journal-Constitution* and intended to stay. The staff wanted more training and understood change was needed to meet audience needs.

But some on the staff were just keeping their heads down. Many of the complaints were typical of newsrooms. Reporters objected to multiple, serial edits on stories; they said they were getting mixed messages. They wanted more discussion and coaching from editors. Staff said poor performers seemed to be tolerated while middle and high performers did not receive sufficient rewards.

We spent three days in the newsroom, interviewing dozens of staff members and attending news meetings. We also reviewed readership and market research and conducted a survey of the newsroom and a content analysis of the newspaper.

Our advice was simple:

- *Leadership.* Newsroom leaders needed to clarify the vision. They needed to be sure their newsroom practices matched the message. Leaders would benefit from communications training.

- *Staff.* Journalists needed to become engaged—in this case, through a training committee—in developing annual goals and the training needed to accomplish them.

"We've had a very aggressive training program," Wallace says. "What (Tomorrow's Workforce) has done is really elevated it and aligned it with our strategic goals."

At the time, the *Journal-Constitution* presented a classic case of an ambitious newspaper with a laundry list of goals. None were journalistically unworthy, but as a set it was nearly impossible for managers and staff to decide which goal was most important on any given day.

During a five-hour discussion in mid-2004, Michele McLellan, director of Tomorrow's Workforce, asked a dozen top *Journal-Constitution* editors to write the answer to the question: "What would make this paper better?" Twenty-five answers later, McLellan asked the group what it thought of its work. "We said, 'Yeah, that's great, yeah, yeah,'" says Wallace. "And she (McLellan) said, 'Well, you can't do all that.' So it forced us into a really good conversation about, OK, what can we do and how do we organize our thoughts around where we're going and really focus our training to match up?"

Eventually, the *Journal-Constitution*'s editors chose three editorial priorities as the pillars—the primary goals—of the 2005 training program: improving beat watchdog reporting, creating greater versatility in storytelling and story form, and making better community connections.

Training director Sheila Garland recruited a staff committee to help convert the goals into training. The result was a yearlong curriculum of nearly 100 training opportunities. "What I would stress," Garland says, "is a team approach to coming up with what you want to learn and aligning your learning strategy with your business goals. It can come from your employees. And, in fact, they're going to participate on a higher level if they're involved from the very beginning—and if they can see a difference in the newspaper."

In 2005, the *Journal-Constitution* published 95 watchdog stories—more than twice as many as the year before—everything from a weeklong series on the lack of consumer protection in Georgia to the revelation of a gambling trip of county officials and developers. Alternative story forms dominated section covers, where they appeared only occasionally the year before. Wallace says brand research showed the paper made real inroads with suburban readers, who now see it as covering the entire metro area, not just the city of Atlanta.

## NEW GOALS FOR A NEW AGE OF JOURNALISM

Many newspapers that have goals, we found, limit them to quality or quantity of journalism—better writing, more stories, fewer errors. Goals like these can be easy to measure.

During the Tomorrow's Workforce project, we used simple content audits to show editors what they were printing every day. Quite often they were surprised. Newspapers that trumpeted a commitment to diversity were sometimes blatantly homogenous. Editors who said they pushed for more people coverage oversaw newspapers engorged with stories about meetings, reports and politics. Newsrooms with written goals to pepper their newspaper with graphics, headlines, teasers and other elements intended to engage readers were devoid of those elements.

The newspapers had measurable goals. But no one was measuring them.

Content goals remain important because doing journalism is a newspaper's primary purpose, but they don't address issues like leadership, planning and understanding audience. For these, newspapers need new goals—and new ways to judge their success.

Dana Robbins, the *Hamilton Spectator* editor, talks of how his standards for success evolved. "When I was city editor," he says, "the *Spectator* won the most number of Ontario newspaper awards that had ever been won in the years of the newspaper. I was sort of cock of the walk. They were nearly all won by city department staff. What a measure of my success as the city editor! The problem with that was while we were winning those awards, the paper was a rag. No exaggeration on that part. By any fair measure, it was a terrible newspaper. It was trashy. It was poorly written. It certainly was not reflective of our readership. Our circulation and readership were plummeting. We were in a death spiral. But that was the year we won the most number of Ontario newspaper awards, and that was the thing I was using as my measure of success."

Robbins' point: "We use metrics to measure our success that oftentimes don't really have a lot to do with readership."

There are harder things to measure, things that today are more important. Robbins asks:

> What are you doing to foster innovation? How are you measuring that? I think that's a really good metric. I'm not taking anything away from journalism awards. We still go after them and I still crow about them. I'm still proud of them. But I spend a lot more time thinking about what are the pieces we have not measured in the past. We do culture surveys, for example, to measure specific cultural attributes in the newsroom and see whether we're achieving them.
>
> If editors tend to think only about journalism, I think that does a tremendous disservice to our newsrooms. If all you're going to do is measure the journalism—and I know that probably sounds like heresy to most editors—but if all you measure is the journalism, then you're probably never going to get a newsroom operating at its fullest potential.

This is about broadening the traditional definitions of journalistic success, such as winning awards, to include measurements that mark progress toward other goals, such as the effect of a newspaper's work on its readers or the number of newsroom innovations put into place.

Newsroom training has suffered from the similarly narrow definition of success.

Unlike most businesses, newspapers do not pay much attention to the money or time they put into professional development, nor do they measure the impact of their training on the newspaper or Web site—not even on classic measurements, like awards. It is no wonder we aren't doing more of it. We cannot really explain what we are putting in and what we are getting out, so how can we justify it? We cannot explain what a businessperson would call the basic ROI—return on investment.

Even newspapers with good training habits, we found, measured success by how much money they spent or the number of people they trained. By themselves, these numbers aren't very helpful. Yet rarely did newspapers look at the effect of the training.

Did sending reporters to conferences on narrative writing and investigative reporting produce more nontraditional stories and more watchdog articles? Did bringing in a consultant to train midlevel editors in time management and better communication actually help them do those things?

We at Tomorrow's Workforce know high-quality, targeted training works, because we have seen the proof: changed journalists and newsrooms; changed newspapers; online innovation; richer, more creative journalism that really reaches people. But we also know that not all training is good training. So journalists need to ask themselves: How do we want to get better? Why? How will we be able to show it worked? When people can see the measurable results of their work, they are encouraged to do more.

Behind this lies what Harvard business scholar John Kotter calls the "central challenge" to change—"people's behavior."

"The central challenge is not strategy, not systems, not culture," says Kotter, ". . . the core problem without question is behavior—what people do, and the need for significant shifts in what people do."[6]

The success of a goal must be determined by its effect on the journalism. And, if the goal also is to influence the audience, their behavior needs to be measured as well. Are they doing what the goal is intended to spur them to do?

## LINKING GOALS, TRAINING AND CHANGE

One lesson from Atlanta and other Tomorrow's Workforce partners is that the combination of focused goals and strategic training can produce desired results. A newspaper that trains without purpose is far less likely to be able to shift a newsroom's direction.

A simple way to link the concepts of goals and training is with the phrase *so that*. Training is about change, about learning something new *so that* a newspaper can transform or improve its journalism.

- Why are we teaching our staff Spanish? *So that* they can connect with our community's fastest growing ethnic population.

- Why are investigative reporting skills important? *So that* we can report with authoritative—and exclusive—knowledge on the institutions that serve our communities.

- Why are we focusing on leadership and communication training for our top editors? *So that* they can lead and motivate their staffs in challenging times.

Training is about learning X *so that* journalists can do Y, and then we expect the audience will do Z. Every discussion on a newspaper about management or editorial goals should naturally lead into a discussion about training—*so that* the staff has the abilities necessary to accomplish those goals.

Melanie Sill, editor of the *News & Observer* in Raleigh, N.C., says training prepares journalists for change and raises the chance of meeting new goals. "We want people to perform new types of work, some of which is not yet defined," she says. "Offering training lowers the fear associated with changing job duties and roles and offers an incentive both for staff members and managers, as training promises to improve the work. Making such demands without offering training seems to guarantee opposition and failure."

Goals focus everyone in the newsroom on the same page. They highlight skills that need to be acquired. They lead to more intentional journalism. They define priorities and let everyone know what is important now. They create ways to measure success—one goal at a time.

## CHAPTER 3

# Newsroom Culture: No More Whining

*Because of a more open workplace, we're getting better stories in the paper.
We're getting more innovation and creativity than we were getting when
everything was running up through a manager. Our circulation is up. That's
really unusual in 2006.*

—Bob Zaltsberg, editor, *The Herald-Times,* Bloomington, Ind.

**C**ontrast two groups of professionals facing an uncertain future. One is defensive. Resists the notion that change and quality are compatible. Beats down new ideas. The other group is constructive. Scans the horizon for new opportunities. Sees the sheer fun of the possibilities ahead.

The former describes a typical newsroom and the newspaper industry as a whole. The latter describes a news organization—still rare but growing in number—that is ready to adapt and thrive in the 21st century.

These are the two faces of workplace culture, a force that shapes "the way we do things around here" in any organization.[1] One face is defensive—risk averse, internally competitive, hierarchically top down, usually so focused on small details of the day-to-day that it loses sight of larger goals—and ultimately unable to keep pace with changing times. The other face is constructive—nimble, collaborative, ready to learn and to try new things, focused on improving the performance of the organization and on each member's achievement—and able to weather fierce competition.

The predominant culture in the newspaper industry is defensive. Newspapers are one of the most defensive workplaces of the thousands experts have measured so far. They are right up there with the military, some hospitals and nuclear power plants. That kind of defensiveness is a powerful barrier to change. Yet news organizations, if they want to reinvent themselves in the 21st century, must change.

When an entire industry reinvents itself, culture must play a key role. Other sectors, banking and retailing, for example, have focused on culture to reinvent themselves. The news industry could draw from their experiences.

This process of change is unfolding in dozens of newsrooms—at *The Atlanta Journal-Constitution* and the *Bakersfield Californian,* for example, as well as in places like the *La Crosse Tribune* in Wisconsin and *The Herald-Times* in Bloomington, Indiana.

This chapter will examine the defensive culture of daily newspapers, how it manifests itself in day-to-day newsroom behavior, and why this matters to journalists, to news executives and to the entire news industry.

The chapter also will explore how strategic training and staff development are helping news organizations build more constructive cultures. In an open newsroom, strategic training can enhance credible, engaging and relevant journalism, even in the face of fundamental shifts in the business model of the industry, the demographics of the news audience and, in some cases, the nature of news.

## WHAT IS CULTURE?

*Culture* is an amorphous term, a touchy-feely sounding concept that seems alien to the hard-charging self-image of the newsroom.

But every organization has a culture, and it controls how individuals think they are expected to behave and how they perform. Even cultures based on misperception and miscommunication remain powerful, persistent collections of common beliefs that dictate behavior within the organization.

John P. Kotter and James L. Heskett of the Harvard Business School define culture as "an interdependent set of values and ways of behaving that are common in a community." The community's beliefs and behaviors "tend to perpetuate themselves, sometimes over long periods of time." Culture comes from "a variety of social forces that are frequently subtle, bordering on invisible," they say, "through which people learn a group's norms and values, are rewarded when they accept them, and are ostracized when they do not."[2]

Culture is the air an organization breathes. It is the environment, unseen but omnipresent, in which everyone works. It helps shape attitudes, morale, values, product and even vocabulary.

Ever see a reporter only a couple of years out of journalism school speak with the same jaded weariness and pessimism as the grizzled, 30-year, seen-it-all cityside reporter? When you do, you know the newcomer has been drinking a potent newsroom Kool-Aid, a daily high-octane shot of defensive culture.

But when both the newcomer and the veteran collaborate with artists or photographers to brainstorm new ways to make local government coverage more engaging and then experiment with their ideas online, something else is at work. Something more constructive.

## WHY DOES CULTURE MATTER TO NEWSPAPERS?

We have known that culture matters for a while. In its landmark Impact Study in 2000, the Readership Institute at Northwestern University in Evanston, Ill., looked at 90 newspapers and found that all but a handful had defensive cultures.

Our own visits to newsrooms confirmed those findings. We saw talented and intelligent journalists balk at changing their ways in the face of an avalanche of evidence that the world is changing. Some flatly equated long enterprise projects with good, serious journalism and rejected shorter material for busy readers as "dumbing down." Some, obsessed with fabled "good old days," blamed editors, owners, Wall Street—even readers—for their loss. Others wondered whether people really cared about news anymore. But could it be that what journalists produce today needs to be more interesting, less repetitive, easier to understand and more useful?

The Readership Institute study also brought good news: newspapers with constructive cultures had stronger readership than the defensive ones.[3] Constructive journalists can help newspapers adapt to changes in audience and technology.

How did the Readership Institute come to focus on culture? According to researchers, for three decades daily newspaper readership had declined "despite extensive research into reader issues and many reader-growth activities at newspapers across the country." Something inside the newspapers seemed to be keeping them from doing the things they knew they should do. "The hypothesis," researchers wrote, "was that culture would be linked ultimately to readership. This, in fact, proved to be the case. Impact research shows that newspapers with constructive cultures tend also to have higher readership."[4]

This was not a revolutionary concept outside the news industry. Experts for decades have linked workforce culture and marketplace success. The Readership Institute noted "echoes . . . from hundreds of studies in other businesses that link the culture of the workplace to employee satisfaction, customer satisfaction and business outcomes, such as profitability and shareholder returns."[5]

The message was clear: change your culture, improve your chances of success.

Any good journalist would at this point find a list of companies that have enjoyed business success with defensive cultures. It is probably a good thing, for example, that the average nuclear power plant does not experiment each day with a new way of containing radiation. The daily newspapers of old were the kinds of business monopolies that could enjoy great profit with a defensive culture. As long as new technology presented no competition and audience preferences did not change, they could always squeeze out a little more.

Enterprises with defensive workplace cultures, such as banking, have some-times thrived for decades, even centuries, without changing their ways. Customers valued authority and a steady hand. But times changed, and so did the banks. The days of Americans waiting 30 minutes in line to cash a check before the bank's midafternoon closing are long gone. Instead, customers have evening and Saturday hours, drive-up windows, electronic banking, ATMs and multiple account options that meet their every need.

Changing a workplace focus from internal to external, from process to cus-tomer, is part of aligning a workplace and its marketplace, say Harvard's Kotter and Heskett. All companies have a marketplace "context," and "strong cultures with practices that do not fit a company's context can actually lead intelligent peo-ple to behave in ways that are destructive—that systematically undermine an orga-nization's ability to survive and prosper."[6]

In other words, a company whose culture is out of step with its audience, its competitors or its sources of income is going to put a lot of well-intentioned effort into doing things that actually harm rather than improve the business.

Newspapers did that for years when they labored to perfect their print product while ignoring ways to reach new readers online. Vickey Williams, director of the Learning Newsroom project, says journalists in general tend to guard the status quo "viciously . . . most often by citing the lack of time to do anything differently."

If ever a culture did not fit its context, it has been the newspaper industry. Household penetration of the home-delivered, daily newspaper has fallen in all industrialized countries since World War II. U.S. households once consumed on average more than one newspaper per day. Now, fewer than half subscribe to a daily newspaper. Yet since the birth of radio, daily newspaper journalists have argued that electronic delivery platforms are inferior in quality.

## UNDERSTANDING AND BREAKING THE DEFENSIVE SHELL

Defensive culture can take either aggressive or passive forms. In-your-face defen-siveness can mean perfectionism to the point of paralysis. It can mean opposi-tional thinking that blocks reform, competitiveness that tears down colleagues. We found ample evidence of it in our hundreds of newsroom interviews. "We dwell on the negative . . . everyone questions everyone else." Behind-your-back defen-siveness can mean people mindlessly following routine. "We self-censor . . . we tell each other as little as possible." Fear of criticism can stifle risk-taking. "People are self-censoring because they are trying to think what the person over them is thinking."

Are we saying that journalists, with their professional futures more uncertain than ever, should not be even a little bit defensive? Of course not. Skepticism is a time-honored journalistic value. Even perfectionism in moderate doses is not undesirable. But when extremes of cynicism and the paralysis of perfectionism set in, they block new ideas. Defensive people see "either-or" choices, not whether there are ways to honor "both." If all efforts to reinvent daily newspaper work are "dumbing down" or "pandering," then there can be no reinvention.

Here is a glimpse of defensive culture at work in the day's news meeting—what one journalist called "the beat down."[7]

A dozen or more editors sit around a conference room table. Section covers from that morning's newspaper are tacked on the wall. The most senior editor opens the meeting with a monolog, lauding a news break in a Page One story, asking why the reporter failed to quote one official in the same story and mentioning that the name of a local athlete was misspelled in the high school sports agate. The city editor adds a few comments about accuracy, deflecting the comment about the missing quote in a story she edited.

By the time the discussion moves to the next day's newspaper, a lot of the early morning energy that came in the door has fled the room. Shields up and heads down, each department representative reads top items from a budget printout, answering the boss as best as possible while fending off questions from peers with a flip answer or a promise to find the answer later.

Even when an editor has a blockbuster in sight, she is reluctant to be pinned down. Editors often have had no conversation or only a passing one with their reporters before the meeting, so they don't really know what they can promise. (Plus the reporters don't want to be pinned down either.) At the same time, word editors labor to deflect questions and suggestions from photography and graphics editors, preferring to keep them out of the loop until they can pry more information out of reporters.

One editor whose team will produce a major story that day says that she will have to pull one or two others off other urgent projects to help. A colleague from another department has at least one reporter at loose ends that day; it does not occur to him to offer help.

With only a vague idea of what the next day's front page will look like, participants escape the conference room. Some feel relieved, others uneasy about what they will be expected to deliver by the end of the day.

What are culture lessons from such a meeting, day after day?

- Low-impact details matter more than high-impact strategies.

- Those who anticipate every possible question will gain approval (and make stories longer so that nothing is left out).

- Peer collaboration is not part of the job description.

- One way to deflect unwanted attention is by questioning others.

- It is better to keep quiet than to take initiative.

- Colleagues are rivals, not partners.

- Fresh ideas will engender skepticism.

No matter that newsroom leaders say they want more risk-taking, more collaboration and more personal initiative, the staff absorbs the more concrete messages of such news meetings and acts accordingly, further hardening the newsroom's defensive shell.

## TABLE 3-1
*Individual Behaviors Influenced by Organizational Cultures*[8]

Cultural norms, as measured by the Organizational Culture Inventory®, reinforce individual thinking and behavioral styles as listed below.

| Constructive | Passive/Defensive | Aggressive/Defensive |
|---|---|---|
| *Achievement* | *Approval* | *Oppositional* |
| Seeks challenging projects | Needs acceptance | Asks tough questions |
| Seeks high-quality results | Tries hard to please others | Emphasizes minor flaws |
| Learns from mistakes | Is obedient | Uses criticism to gain attention |
| *Self-actualizing* | *Conventional* | *Power* |
| Displays desire to learn | Conforms | Dictates (rather than guides) others' actions |
| Is a creative yet realistic thinker | Avoids calling attention to self | Treats others in forceful ways |
| | Prefers the status quo | |
| *Humanistic-encouraging* | *Dependent* | *Competitive* |
| Interested in growth of others | *Self-protective* | Protects status by outperforming others |
| Coaches, counsels others | Allows others to make decisions for one | Views noncompetitive situations as contests |
| *Affiliative* | *Avoidance* | *Perfectionistic* |
| Seeks positive relationships | Plays it safe | Preoccupied with details |
| Is friendly and cooperative | Minimizes risks | Places excessive demands on self and others |
| | Shies away from group activity and discussion | |

Imagine a different meeting, one in which editors share fledgling ideas and peers encourage them. One that assesses the day's newspaper and online report against strategic goals and assigns resources to priorities everyone understands.

Changing culture is more complicated than just changing the news meeting.

You can't transform a workplace merely by telling everyone to change. That's why leadership and goals have to change first. Industrial psychologist Pierre Meyer says real culture change takes three to five years of intensive, hard work and constant attention:

> There are many elements to it, and each element requires time for adaptation and adjustment. In a simplistic way, the change process begins with understanding how current work is accomplished. Which systems and processes is an organization currently using? Those systems and processes are wedded to our beliefs about work and ourselves. Our beliefs lead us to an understanding of current reality and that reality leads us to current work behaviors. Before we can begin the process of change, we need to re-think those beliefs, realities and behaviors.

Most people are more comfortable with present behaviors and styles than they are with the thought or the reality of change. They are resistant to change.

## HOW TO CHANGE NEWSROOM CULTURE

Culture change is possible. Newsrooms that are working to improve their cultures are doing three basic things:

- Offering more training and more strategic training, a key byproduct of which is better communication.

- Employing groups such as staff committees to identify problems and recommend solutions.

- Allowing more decision making—and trial-and-error—at the staff level.

As we stated in chapter 1, top newsroom executives must let go of the day-to-day news production and focus on the future. Editor Zaltsberg, for example, learned about one new blog only after it had been launched:

> Two years ago that would have made me feel really uncomfortable. Now we've done enough talking about what we want and the readership we're going after, I trust that they'll do a good job. If they don't, we'll worry about it later.

Interestingly, this transfer of responsibility seems to give staff not just greater engagement in the news but also in the paper's future. Mike Jenner, executive editor of the *Bakersfield Californian,* saw the culture of his newsroom go from the typical defensive profile to the cusp of constructive in 18 months:

> One of the hardest things we've had to do—and it's not just me, but my department heads and all the managers here—is letting go. We're such control freaks. Getting things right is critical to our credibility, but the idea that I've got to sign off on it, or I've got to be the last guy to touch it, that tends to tell people below us that "I don't need to worry about this so much." Learning to tell people "this is yours, you're in charge, I'm not going to follow up," that's really vital to reaching a level where people feel they are empowered to innovate and to take risks.

Like many editors, Jenner says, "we've got many, many smart people in this newsroom." But he adds that they don't need him constantly looking over their shoulder. "Some of the old habits I learned from editors I worked for over the years, I have to let go of those because I think they're detrimental."

Editors can break down newsroom defenses by putting a newspaper's goals on the table and talking about them often. A key goal should be better communication. This can help stop people from withholding information as a way to try to assert power, or of using the claim of confusion as a passport to do whatever they want.

Explains Meyer, the industrial psychologist:

> Communication processes and systems are central to culture and to culture change. Poor communications are exemplified by closed systems, hierarchical structures, "silo-ed" departments or units, competition that undermines collaboration, and dependence upon rumor rather than use of formal and informal purposeful dissemination. These are signs of a defensive culture.
>
> A crucial hallmark of constructive cultures is transparency—the degree to which all know the strategic intent of the organization and all have a chance to raise questions and make comments.

Says Zaltsberg, the Bloomington editor:

> The first thing good culture includes is better communication. There's just more information that's shared with everybody. Today, we're having a brown bag meeting about the newsroom budget. We'll talk about how it's put together, what our revenue goals are—and we're not meeting them, which is why we're not filling a position.

## STAFF ENGAGEMENT, CULTURE AND TRAINING

All transitions, especially leadership transitions, leave an awkward void, a space that no one quite knows how to fill. Newsroom committees are an important vehicle for promoting staff engagement. Not the old model of a committee led by executives with a few star journalists, but one that reflects the newsroom and one that may take a while to figure out what to do.

"We kind of floundered, asking, 'How are we supposed to do this?'" says Bethany Nolan, a reporter and committee member at *The Herald-Times* in Bloomington. But within a year, Bloomington committees created a newsroom-training program, initiated discussions of beat restructuring and freed up the company information it needed about Web traffic to help build a stronger online presence. Newsroom culture (measured by standard workplace culture tests) improved. Nolan called the Learning Newsroom process "a life-changing experience that has ruffled some feathers in our newsroom. But in the end I think that it will make—and has made—great changes."

In Tomorrow's Workforce newsrooms, members of training committees—like the *Atlanta* committee described in chapter 2—explore goals with newsroom executives, explain the goals to their peers and ask them what training they would need to meet them. When thinking about culture, the committee is a key element that improves communication and staff engagement in both goals and learning. It also allows the leadership to tap into a leadership cadre that is not always visible from the corner office.

As we will see in the next chapter, training coworkers together is a powerful way to effect change in news content and in newsroom culture. It is vital to opening communications among coworkers and across newsroom silos.

The Learning Newsroom developed a five-part curriculum that encompasses learning priorities for newsrooms that want to improve culture:

- *Communication.* Efforts to make communication more honest, direct and meaningful for individual and team performance.

- *Business literacy.* A better understanding of the strategies of the newspaper and how the work of all departments—newsroom, advertising, marketing and circulation—contributes to the enterprise.

- *Innovation.* An overview of ways in which organizations are identifying opportunities and responding with new products.

- *Systems analysis.* Looking at current practices, suggesting more effective ones.

- *Time management.* Exercises to help staff discover time-consuming practices that may no longer be efficient or necessary and stop or modify them.

These Learning Newsroom modules, with committee work, improved newsroom culture in most of the newsrooms where the project operated.

Good training that deals with the newsroom as a group can produce positive culture change, even when the specific topic is not newsroom culture itself. For the past few years, the Committee of Concerned Journalists has offered "critical thinking" modules to groups of 25 to 40 journalists in more than 200 newsrooms. Seventy-five percent of the participants said newsroom communications—chiefly teamwork and information sharing—had improved because of these workshops.[9] That benefit came on top of whatever else was to be learned, such as increasing enterprise reporting or connecting better with the community.

William Damon, a professor of education at Stanford University, and Brett Mueller, his research associate, conducted follow-up interviews to assess the impact of the training. They wrote:

> [T]he most frequent reported benefit of our training was "improved communications" with co-workers up and down the ranks, with several interviewees in every newsroom stating that it was their favorite outcome of the workshop.
>
> This finding was especially noteworthy to us because communication was more of a sub-text than a text, embedded in the way we arranged the small-group discussions and other collaborative exercises—discussions and exercises focused on the elements and tools of journalism.[10]

## "THINGS MAY GET WORSE BEFORE THEY GET BETTER"

Here is an understatement: Not everyone in a newsroom takes to culture change quickly or readily. Some may charge ahead. Many may look on in curiosity. Others may resist—hard and loud. "There's still opposition . . . to doing anything new and inventive as a whole," one journalist said months into a culture-change regimen. "Some won't budge and I simply feel that their negative vibes aren't helping us a whole lot."[11]

Nolan, the reporter in Bloomington, says nearly two years after the culture-change program began that the gap between enthusiasts and resisters is more evident. This worries her: "I see a greater divide between staffers who are sold on what we can do and those who are naysayers." Says Williams, the Learning Newsroom project director: "This work really kicks up the dust and things may get worse before they get better."

After its first year, *The Hamilton Spectator*'s committee worried:

> The learning newsroom process has succeeded in deeply engaging a small core of staff in the process of change and regeneration . . . but the majority remain on the sidelines, intent on and very busy with their daily business, pausing now and again to throw the odd rock or flower as the spirit moves them . . . the "engaged core" is burning out from the burden of shifting an isolationist newsroom away from its defensive/aggressive habits.[12]

Dana Robbins, editor of the *Spectator*, recalls a newsroom-wide staff meeting to discuss the amount of change at the newspaper. The paper had radically restructured even before its participation in the Learning Newsroom project, killing sections, starting new ones and rearranging staff. "We had gone through huge turmoil here with the amount of change we've had," Robbins says.

At the meeting, Learning Newsroom leaders asked, "Hands up. How many of you think the *Spectator* has embraced too much change, is changing too quickly?" About 40 percent of the staff raised their hands, Robbins remembers, some of them quite aggressively, as though saying, "You're damn right! Too much change!" Then they asked, "How many of you think the *Spectator* is not changing fast enough?" About another 40 percent raised their hands.

In fact, the staff was told, a survey had shown that "the youngest talent . . . were not only saying we were not changing fast enough, but they'd actually considered leaving the *Spectator* if we did not change more." Robbins looked around.

"You know I'm an old-timer," he says. "I've been here forever, I'm part of the furniture. . . . I could see the shock on their faces. They just couldn't comprehend that there was this group of people in their midst that were saying, 'You need to change even more.'"

## TRAINING AND THE *CORPUS CHRISTI CALLER-TIMES*

When Vice President Dick Cheney accidentally shot a fellow hunter on a Texas ranch in 2006, the local *Corpus Christi Caller-Times* broke a story that made national headlines.

Understandably, staff members of the 51,000-circulation newspaper congratulated themselves for beating the national news media to the story. Surprisingly, they credited a training program. The Cheney story brought home how much their participation in a year's worth of culture-change training had ignited their initiative and strengthened their teamwork.

"The quick response, the innovations in multimedia, the deliberate approach to covering the story are all hallmarks of the (Learning Newsroom) program," says reporter Neal Falgoust. "Had this story happened two years ago, I think we would have had a much more fragmented reaction from the top." [13]

An old school response to a big story on a small paper would be for top editors to call in the whole staff, then rush to the paper to run the show. Instead, says editor Libby Averyt, on this Sunday in February the staff just went ahead and mapped out its Page One coverage and put the news online. Later the staff created a video demonstration firing the type of weapon Cheney used.

Averyt learned of the shooting when she turned on her cell phone as she left a matinee of Woody Allen's film "Match Point." She called Managing Editor Shane Fitzgerald, who had been in touch with the newsroom and knew what the staff was planning. Averyt headed to an art exhibit; Fitzgerald decided he didn't need to go into the newsroom either.

Newsroom traditionalists may find this a startling and undesirable departure from the editor-as-commander approach. But Averyt saw it as an essential step toward her goal of developing a staff that seized the initiative. For the staff to step up, she and Fitzgerald had decided, they would need to step back. "They didn't need me breathing down their necks," Averyt says.

Six months later, the effort to build a better culture was alive. "More ideas are coming to the table," says Michelle Christenson Parker, a photographer and member of the newsroom steering committee. "People are more interested and trying to get involved. We push people to get involved."

*Caller-Times* journalists were busily working on content aimed at teenagers and young adults online and in print. The staff recruited a youth advisory board and gave members free subscriptions for six months in exchange for critiquing the newspaper. "When you're in a newsroom you get tunnel vision," Parker says. "We have to step out of ourselves and really find out what people are interested in instead of assuming we know. In the past it's been about us and not about them."

They also were hard at work on improving communications. A new system corrects errors online more quickly. Another encourages online editors to meet individually with reporters to establish online goals for each. Editors were trained on time management and how to have effective meetings. It really helped, Parker says, when staff members took the Myers-Briggs Type Inventory, which measures personality type, and posted their results:

> Everybody doesn't talk about things the same way or like to be talked to in the same way. You start to realize why you have a hard time communicating with someone. We're not butting heads, we just have a different style of communication. It makes you think more about how you deliver messages and talk about things to have the most effective communication.

Kathryn Garcia, the reporter who got the call about the Cheney shooting, says she noticed major shifts in attitudes during the first year of the Learning Newsroom program. People were really negative, lots of harping, she says:

> It wasn't that way all the time, but there was a lot of complaining about work. Now I don't hear that. . . . I think now there's really been a dramatic change that went from thinking of ourselves as solitary workhorses to (thinking) that we're a team. . . .

The Corpus Christi newsroom saw its constructive behavior increase markedly as a result of the project. People outside the Corpus Christi newsroom noticed. Ron Ferriby, the newspaper's vice president for production, says the newspaper's on-time press start record was nearly perfect after missing one in 10 deadlines the year before. "They've taken time to listen to every department and they've taken bigger ownership in the total production of the paper," Ferriby says. "We're really moving."

## STRATEGIC TRAINING PRODUCES MEASURABLE RESULTS

As three out of four newsrooms trained by the Committee of Concerned Journalists reported better communications, most Learning Newsroom and Tomorrow's Workforce newsrooms showed better culture scores.

Of 13 highly active newsrooms where cultural surveys were administered before training began and again about 18 months later,[14] 10 showed consistent improvement—starting to move away from defensive behavior. The culture of three others overall was largely unchanged; however, the most heavily trained group in two newsrooms—the middle managers—did show progress.

Meyer analyzed the results. Though early—just a third of the way through the expected change period of up to five years—they are promising. "The results so far . . . clearly show important positive change," he says. "Most of the newsrooms appear to be on the right track and likely will continue to change. A few appear less likely to move to a new culture unless efforts intensify."

The Bloomington newsroom was among those that improved. Editor Zaltsberg emphasizes the notion that change had just begun: "There are fewer and fewer people in that group of nonbelievers. Our culture makes it uncomfortable for people who don't want to change."

Zaltsberg attributes an 8 percent increase in single-copy sales to the culture work, willingness to innovate and more decision making from the ranks. "Part of it is we have a very aggressive readership plan that everybody knows about and everybody understands," he says.

Change was evident in shifting attitudes.[15] Some people felt renewed and ready to work again: "It was very exciting to, essentially, hit the restart button on so many things we do here," they said. "Never again will 'that's the way we've always done it' be an adequate explanation. We now have the tools—and the permission—to keep doing better." Others began collaborating with their bosses: "I now can talk with superiors; they are open to ideas and to conversation." And others saw the whole newsroom in context: "We're better at deadlines because of process improvements. There's also more awareness of why it's important."

Each partner newsroom lists a dozen or more outcomes that reflect staff-driven solutions to newsroom problems, some that immediately improved the news product and others that streamlined processes or made them more open. At *The Hamilton Spectator* in Ontario, Canada, for example, an "Innovation Time Bank" gives every newsroom staff member a shot at stepping away from routine duties for up to 80 hours a year to work on entrepreneurial ideas that management believes have a high potential for serving readers.

Is it risky to embark on such open-ended journeys, to offer journalists time off from their regular work to brainstorm something that may or may not ever get into the newspaper? Is it even riskier to take on a five-year process of culture and communication change, with only a general sense that things will be better? Sure. But given the digital revolution, aren't there even greater risks for those who do not innovate?

## CHAPTER 4

# The Well-Balanced Learning Diet

*The economy will continue to be volatile. Technology is changing so fast. Learning is constant. There doesn't seem to be any end to this. We have to get used to the idea that the end point is never going to happen. You've got to have a learning culture because you may have a strategy now and a vision now that in a year you may have to completely revamp.*

— Monica Moses, executive director of product innovation, Minneapolis *Star Tribune*

The news industry trains people as badly as a fast-food diet nourishes them. Training is episodic rather than continuous. Random, rather than strategic. Long on talk. Short on measurable impact. Not exactly the kind of well-balanced learning diet Monica Moses envisions.

In the course of the Tomorrow's Workforce project, we developed a "learning pyramid" modeled on the traditional food pyramid that illustrates a healthy diet. Our pyramid is designed to help news organizations envision a strategic framework for their newsroom-training programs. The pyramid encourages more goal-oriented training and more group training, things that we are convinced help journalists produce the intended results. This chapter will explain the learning pyramid. We will show how some newsrooms have used its concepts to build stronger, more effective training programs. We will also look at lessons from other industries and list key steps for developing your own program without breaking the bank.

## FOUNDATION LEVEL: WHAT EVERYONE NEEDS TO KNOW

At the top of the learning pyramid is the journalist—an editor, a photographer, an artist or a reporter—learning something new about craft, or topic knowledge, or ethics, or professional management techniques.

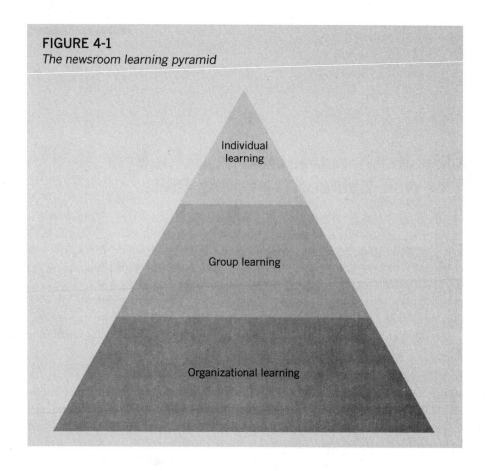

**FIGURE 4-1**
*The newsroom learning pyramid*

Individual learning

Group learning

Organizational learning

In the middle are groups of journalists, the copy desk or metro reporters, or a mix of disciplines. These are teams that learn common skills and apply them together.

At the bottom is the whole newsroom, all departments, everyone from the executive editor to the news aide. This is where organizational learning occurs.

Newsroom learning is what everyone is working on together—newsroom-wide priorities—whether it is ethics, diversity, watchdog reporting or more engaging ways of telling stories. As the foundation of all newsroom training, it supports strategic goals and provides the context for individual training. Newsroom-wide learning also proclaims a newspaper's standards. It is a way of expressing, "This is how we do journalism here. We are all going to have this knowledge and these skills, and we're going to apply them routinely to our work."

Organizational learning is a minimum daily requirement for the adaptive, constructive newsroom. It stresses affirmative practices, builds common experiences and vocabulary and provides opportunities for collaboration that chip away at the defensive shell of the newsroom.

Yet most journalism training today tends to focus on individuals. Reporters, for example, learn new writing skills, but their editors don't necessarily learn how to help them write better. This type of training creates silos. Disconnected skill levels vary widely across the newsroom. The staff cannot pull in one direction.

Whole newsroom training enables people to develop a common language, so they know and understand exactly what their goals mean and how to achieve them. For example:

- If the goal is to bring more diverse voices into the news report, classes help all journalists learn about communities beyond the traditional focus of the newsroom. This includes frontline editors, copy editors, reporters, columnists and photographers.

- If the goal is to produce more content for online, classes might help everyone in the newsroom understand differences in audience preferences or storytelling techniques between print and online.

- If the goal is to ensure that the staff understands how to use the Freedom of Information Act, classes might detail the act's major provisions so that everyone knows what is possible (while offering additional hands-on training for those who use it directly).

In Minneapolis, the *Star Tribune* used the "what everyone needs to know" approach in advance of a major redesign in the fall of 2005. Editors scheduled multiple sessions with staff at intervals as they planned the redesign. Managing Editor Scott Gillespie and Monica Moses, then a deputy managing editor, led the sessions.

They detailed plans and rationales, showed samples of new formats, described new beats and took questions. The editors followed up by distributing "Story Forms at the *Star Tribune*," a rich, 57-page guide—created by the staff—that described more than 20 story forms and when they might be used to advantage.

The *Star Tribune*'s emphasis on training added to the burden to senior editors, who were already overloaded with the redesign work and management of the daily newspaper. But Moses says training was critical to the project's success.

The redesign went far beyond a routine change in the look and feel of the *Star Tribune*. It emphasized changes in thinking about beats and stories as well as new design formats. The time for training, Moses says, created space for reflection, questioning and learning that would not have been possible in the daily rush of production.

For me, training is more of a creative group process. As a group we're trying to figure it out. . . .

I think if you really want change, you have to create a time and a space for that discussion. We did all this training with our redesign. You can really track the changes of mind.

Early on in this module, I had a quote from somebody who talked about the readership crisis. I asked the group: 'Who here thinks today's readership crisis is overblown?' Most hands went up. In training six months later, a lot more people believed there is a crisis.

At minimum, activities like these give journalists an understanding of goals and formats, and a chance to react and ask questions. This training helps journalists understand the context in which they work. It gives the newsroom a common vocabulary with commonly understood definitions; it improves communication and, ultimately, performance.

So when the newsroom's top editors want more watchdog journalism, the steps can be set out clearly. Perhaps they will improve spot enterprise from local government beats by looking at public documents more regularly and more deeply. Perhaps they will more often look for unique stories rather than producing so many "meeting stories." Perhaps the reporters will better understand the importance of visuals in helping people understand data-laden pieces and collaborate more effectively.

Managers can extend this learning with follow-up conversations in working groups or with individuals about what the goals mean to their jobs and what needs to be learned to accomplish the goals. This sets the stage for the next level of the pyramid.

## SECOND LEVEL: LEARNING AND WORKING TOGETHER

Moving up the pyramid, next comes group training.

Group learning deepens the individual skills of journalists and improves their ability to work together to reach their goals. It also helps them learn better from each other.

Most group training in newsrooms occurs with traditional department boundaries. Copy editors learn about grammar and headlines, reporters attend sessions on narrative writing and interviewing, photographers are trained in the latest technology. All this makes a good deal of sense: peer-to-peer learning and discipline-specific training are important. If this is the only group training a newsroom does, however, the program is incomplete. It reinforces the silo effect in the newsroom—the sense that each job is separate rather than part of the whole.

Copy editors, for example, know how to work with other copy editors. But they are less equipped to communicate with reporters or photographers. Inside their silos, copy editors, reporters, photographers and managers can get mired in the "us vs. them" mode of defensive newsroom culture.

Cross-disciplinary training, another building block of organizational learning, can demolish those silos and improve performance of the entire newsroom.

For example:

- Training in storytelling will have more impact if writers, line and copy editors, photographers, artists and designers learn together, air their varying perspectives, understand each other's sensibilities and apply the learning together in actual work.

- Training frontline editors about their growing and increasingly demanding roles in the newsroom will be more effective if their bosses and staffs hear the lessons as well.

- Training reporters to gather audio and video for the Web will be more effective if their supervisors also participate. Then the bosses can understand what it takes to get the work done—even if they themselves are not expected to do it. (Since most editors in the newsrooms of 2006 have not come up through the ranks in an online newsroom, how else will they become familiar with the time needs, the best practices, the ethical pitfalls and the journalistic challenges staff may encounter?)

- Training senior editors to better communicate through words and actions as individuals and in cohesive groups. This will help staff hear a common message rather than a mix of priorities.

*The Atlanta Journal-Constitution* recognized this importance of cross-disciplinary training in discussions of a major goal: varying storytelling forms. Traditionally, the goal might have been better writing, with storytelling as a subset. But in today's news media, visual elements—and a skillful marriage of art and word—make writing a subset of good storytelling.

*Atlanta*'s aim was to move away from the dominant traditional news story and encourage use of more creative and engaging story forms that increase readership.

"Writers, editors, designers, copy editors and artists were represented from every department in the alternative storytelling classes. Students overwhelmingly gave the session a thumbs-up," says Sheila Garland, director of newsroom training at AJC.

*Atlanta* could measure the impact of its training. On Page One, the traditional inverted pyramid style story had dominated—with about two-thirds of all stories using that form. By early 2006, nearly 60 percent of the stories were told in nontraditional ways.

"There has not only been an increase in the use of ASFs—the new acronym for 'alternative story forms' that's become jargon in the last year or so—throughout the paper, but an interest expressed by many to do even more and find even better ways to present information," Garland says.

*Atlanta* also provided two days of training exclusively for its 100 frontline editors in 2004, geared to helping them understand their changing roles in the newsroom and identify necessary skill sets.

In 2005, at the request of its newsroom training committee, noneditors were participating in the training as well.

"One of the big ideas that came out (of the *AJC* training committee) . . . is having training as much as possible that involves both the reporters and the editors," says Ty Tagami, a local government reporter. "Because a lot of us have been off to Poynter or IRE. And then you come back, and they want the same old thing. The language isn't there to communicate even."

The South Florida *Sun-Sentinel* is experimenting with a different form of editor-with-reporter training. The newsroom's "learning cell" project brings writing coach Mary Ann Hogan together each week with a reporter and editor over a period of months to discuss story ideas and forms. City Hall reporter Brittany Wallman, one of about a dozen participants in the first nine months, laughingly calls it "marriage counseling for reporters and editors."

The program, which began in 2006, has yielded more engaging news content (one effort won first place in a state journalism competition) and improved teamwork and communication.

The effort also appears to be injecting new excitement into a newsroom that is particularly busy—with print competitors on two sides and a burgeoning multimedia function.

"I've been to a lot of training," Wallman says. "But this has been the most effective to really achieve results."

## THIRD LEVEL: INDIVIDUAL LEARNING

The next step up the learning pyramid from group training is the individual journalist. This training, which may take place in the newsroom or off-site, emphasizes individual interests and needs. For example, a writer who wants to improve certain techniques or a photographer who wants to learn more about lighting will get these individually focused sessions. Training for underperformers may be part of the mix, but the program should take care to give the most training to those most likely to improve, usually middle or high performers.

Individual choices are informed and often influenced by a deeper understanding from the newsroom-wide and group training. These individuals already are aware of where the organization is going and what it will take for them to contribute successfully within the new vision. They are honing their skills to make the final product just that much better.

Take, for example, a reporter who wants to develop her narrative voice. She might go to a training session and learn a great deal about reporting and writing the long narrative. Or, knowing the newspaper wants to infuse narrative techniques in shorter daily stories, she might make that part of her learning agenda for the workshop as well.

Newsroom goals can also help set priorities for individual training when resources are scarce. A newsroom that wants to increase its database enterprise stories might send one computer-assisted reporting editor to a seminar to become an effective trainer, rather than sending two or three investigative reporters to a conference that year.

This tier also includes training that typically requires a dollar investment to send the participant off-site. One such category would be specialized topic knowledge—religion, ethics, science, etc. Another category would be where a significant skill is learning to interact with peers from around the country: high-end writing and frontline editing, for example, or training that works best with immersion, such as computer-assisted reporting.

In summary, instead of disconnected, sporadic training sessions that don't consistently drive change and improve the journalistic product, the pyramid is a framework for a training program that is continuous and has many interlocking pieces and the capacity to create significant results. It is the vehicle that aligns newsroom goals and learning.

## ORGANIZATIONAL LEARNING AND ALIGNMENT WITH GOALS

Training across newsroom disciplines will help foster what learning expert Peter M. Senge calls "'alignment,' when a group of people function as a whole."

"The fundamental characteristic of the relatively unaligned team is wasted energy. Individuals may work extraordinarily hard, but their efforts do not efficiently translate to team effort," Senge says. With more alignment "there is less wasted energy," he says. "In fact, a resonance or synergy develops, like the coherent light of a laser rather than the incoherent and scattered light of a light bulb. There is commonality of purpose, a shared vision, and understanding of how to complement one another's efforts."[1] In other words, newspapers, like any organization, will accomplish more if their staff members work with singular focus on common strategic goals. And time-pressed newsrooms can gain long-term efficiency if they first pause to examine their goals and standards and learn a common language for them in the process.

**TABLE 4-1**
*Shifting Training Paradigms in Old and New Newsrooms*

|  | Old training paradigm | 21st-century learning paradigm |
|---|---|---|
| Place | Building | On demand |
| Content | Upgrade technical skills | Build core competencies |
| Methodology | Learn by listening | Action learning |
| Audience | Individual | Teams |
| Lead faculty | Professors, consultants | Senior managers |
| Frequency | One-time event | Continuous learning |
| Goal | Build individual skills | Solve business issues and improve job performance |

Of course, "alignment" and workplace culture, which we discussed in the previous chapter, are highly compatible and even synergistic. In constructive cultures, colleagues balance considerable drive for individual achievement with a deep understanding and support for the goals and success of the team.

Other industries attempted to enhance such alignment in the 1980s and 1990s, which saw the Corporate University become a common fixture. Jeanne C. Meister, an organizational development expert who has studied hundreds of U.S. companies, says the transformation of American industry into a global knowledge industry brought significant changes to training—not the least of which was a shift in focus from teaching individual employees to teaching work teams together:[2]

> A growing number of companies have begun to perceive a need to shift the focus of their training and corporate education efforts from one-time training events in a classroom that builds individual skills to creating a continuous learning culture where employees learn from each other and share innovations and best practices with an eye toward solving real business issues.[3]

Table 4-1 is adapted from material from Meister.[4]

From her research, Meister distilled a list of "core" competencies that employers were seeking in a global marketplace. Interestingly, the capacity to learn topped the list:[5]

1. Learning to learn

2. Communication and collaboration

3. Creative thinking and problem-solving

4. Technological literacy

5. Global business literacy

6. Leadership development

7. Career self-management

The list has resonance in today's news industry in transition. In addition to being a good journalist—with all the judgment and skill that job requires—today's reporter, photographer or senior editor must constantly find out new ways to do the work, must work as part of a team to solve problems, must keep up to date with technology and the information marketplace, must develop her capacity to lead and to perform.

## RESOURCES

*Training is just essential. We can't move forward and create an open idea culture and have a newsroom where people make changes and try bold things without training them to think and act that way.*

John Smalley, editor, *La Crosse (Wis.) Tribune*

It takes resources to bring continuous learning to the newsroom. But it may not take as much money as budget-conscious journalists imagine.

The future of newsroom training lies within the news organization. While destination training centers like The Poynter Institute and the American Press Institute play a valuable role in providing off-site training for targeted groups of journalists, the economics of modern newsgathering and the necessity for broader, group-focused learning point to a need for more in-house training.

*The Atlanta Journal-Constitution* provides a good example. At the *AJC* journalists can use the newsroom intranet to enroll in nearly 100 in-house training offerings. The staff, which is expected to complete 20 to 30 hours of training every year, also may request training away from the newsroom or take an online class at Poynter's News University.

The bounty of opportunities suggests a training budget that might equal the payroll of a small newspaper. But *Atlanta* more than doubled the amount of training between 2003 and 2005 without significantly increasing direct spending— about $45,000 annually, on training, roughly $100 per journalist on staff.

Instead, editor Julia Wallace and her staff focused on a resource over which they had control: time.

"The time and focus is the real resource, not the money," Wallace says.

Working with Tomorrow's Workforce, *Atlanta* grew its training hours by using more in-house experts as trainers and bringing outside trainers to the newsroom to train groups rather than sending people away for training. In 2003, for example, about half of *Atlanta*'s 4,000 training hours were spent at national and regional sites. In 2005, only one in 10 hours took staff members off-site. Figure 4-2 shows how *AJC* allocated its training hours in 2005, compared to 2003.

In 2003, nearly all of *AJC*'s training dollars went to sending people away for training. In 2005, about 15 percent of the dollars went for training away from the newsroom. Three quarters of the budget went to bringing trainers to the newsroom, many for cross-disciplinary sessions.

And what about the small newsroom with commensurably less budget and not as deep a newsroom bench? The *La Crosse (Wis.) Tribune* spent virtually its entire $3,000 training budget sending people away for training in 2004. In 2005, it nearly tripled its dollar commitment, still a modest $11,000, and used about half to send people away and half to bring experts to the newsroom. *La Crosse* also got help hosting a conference on readership from its corporate parent, Lee Enterprises, Inc.

This is not to suggest the money isn't important. As we will discuss further in chapters 6 and 7, news industry investment in training lags far behind other industries. But newsroom executives should not let money be an excuse not to put forth the effort to develop training programs. The shortage of training has and will cost the industry in the long run in the currency of readers and relevance.

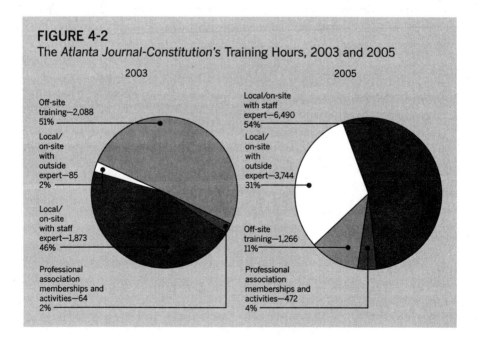

**FIGURE 4-2**
The *Atlanta Journal-Constitution*'s Training Hours, 2003 and 2005

2003

Off-site
training—2,088
51%

Local/
on-site
with
outside
expert—85
2%

Local/
on-site
with staff
expert—1,873
46%

Professional
association
memberships and
activities—64
2%

2005

Local/on-site
with staff
expert—6,490
54%

Local/
on-site
with
outside
expert—3,744
31%

Off-site
training—1,266
11%

Professional
association
memberships and
activities—472
4%

# TRAINING FROM WITHIN: A TALE OF TWO NEWSROOMS

*We think that an effective training program makes maximum use of the resources
your newsroom already has. It's a lot more efficient and you have a lot more
control of the schedule, of the content and, in some cases, the quality than when
you ask an outside person.*

—George Rede, director of recruiting and training, *The Oregonian*

*The Oregonian* and the *Gaston Gazette* could not be more different newspapers. The
*Gazette* sells 32,000 newspapers a day, *The Oregonian* 325,000. The *Gazette* has a
newsroom staff of 36, *The Oregonian* more than 300.

What the *Gazette* and *The Oregonian* do share, though, is a deep, institutional
belief that journalists need ongoing training and that often the best people to provide it are their own fellow editors, reporters, photographers and artists.

Oregonian University emerged in 2002 as an entity that pulled together all the
ad hoc training happening at *The Oregonian*. In its first two years, Oregonian U
sponsored more than 150 training activities: classes, brown bags, workshops, field
trips. Significantly, more than a third of those events featured speakers from *The
Oregonian* staff, ranging from managing editors to graphic artists.

A few examples show the range:

- Two reporters—a suburban reporter and a business reporter—do an hour-
  long workshop on what they learned at the (IRE) convention. The suburban
  reporter also visits all five suburban bureaus with a modified version of the
  program, ensuring that bureau staffs don't get left out (a common complaint at many papers).

- Several copy editors present a video made "to show people in a very fun way
  how copy flows from reporter to line editor and then where it goes from
  there before it finally lands in the paper." The video is a takeoff on *Oregonian*
  reporter Richard Read's Pulitzer Prize–winning article "French Fry
  Connection," which traces the route of a potato around the world. "We followed a potato here," says George Rede, the newsroom training coordinator,
  "which represented a story as it went through the production process, the
  'Copy Desk Connection.'"

- Steve Engelberg, managing editor/enterprise, offers sessions on how to write
  a nut graph and how to write a bright. "How to write a nut graph filled the
  room," says Rede.

At the much smaller *Gazette* in Gastonia, N.C., editor John Pea decided his main
training resource was he himself.

Pea devised a lengthy training program for his newsroom managers after he took over the paper. He says he found that "it had a lot of editors who were good at editing—you know the story—they were good at editing; but dealing with people, doing performance issues, the basics, they really hadn't had any instruction on at all."

"Lacking any other available resources," Pea relied on his experiences, the advice of others and, occasionally, the local public library, and built a syllabus that contained seven sections. (Two examples are "Leadership vs. Management" and "Getting the Job Done.") He created 40 one-hour classes on topics that range from coaching to hiring to personal accountability.

Pea worked with three of his managers at a time throughout the program, which borrowed from Pea's own background, an extensive reading list of popular management books like "Fatal Errors Managers Make" and "The One Minute Manager," and numerous other role-playing and hands-on exercises.

"What I had hoped to do," says Pea, referring to the readings he assigned his editors, "was to get the ideas flowing, to get them thinking. . . . We used (the sessions) as the time to discuss it and try to point out what I wanted to make sure they got out of it."

Pea receives three layers of benefits from his approach to training: one strategic, another financial and the third personal.

"It helped me mold my editors the way I wanted them," says Pea, "and, second, it was a lot cheaper to do. . . . I also became a better editor, because I was scouring everywhere to come up with the best resources, the best reads, the best activities to do in conjunction with this. So, I improved myself in the process."

When a newspaper embraces training as a strategic necessity, it is a natural ensuing step to use its own reporters, editors, photographers and artists as primary sources of journalistic know-how. They know the paper best, they hold the trust of their colleagues and, of course, they are already paid for.

Befitting an editor who couldn't think of a reason why he shouldn't train his staff himself, Pea aptly summarizes the thinking of those journalists who can do—and still teach:

> First, just decide you've got to do it and that you can't use the excuse of no time or no expertise. I just pulled together various resources to get me the expertise. It's more commitment of time than anything else.

Tomorrow's Workforce partner newsrooms consistently demonstrated that training would happen if the top editors want it to happen and the top editors were willing to devote time and energy to creating and maintaining a program. Where leadership attention drifted, so did training; where leaders stayed engaged, training happened. It was about choice; the time—even money—followed.

## 10 STEPS TO A NEWSROOM LEARNING PROGRAM

Just as cultural change is hard, time-consuming work, so is the shift from a random, individual-focused training to an approach that is both strategic and comprehensive. The newsroom staffs that invested the time and energy as part of Tomorrow's Workforce say the effort was worth it, especially after they measure results and see culture and content begin to improve.

In looking at some of our more successful partners (and we defined success as improvement in newsroom culture and news content), we distilled a list of essential elements in building an effective learning program, or Newsroom University:

1. Keep the newsroom's goals out front.

2. Put someone in charge.

3. Engage the staff.

4. Illustrate specific goals.

5. Know the newsroom, know the market.

6. Identify trainers and develop modules.

7. Clarify expectations for attendance and participation.

8. Create a long-range training calendar.

9. Consider quality of training.

10. Measure impact of training.

### Keep the Newsroom's Goals Out Front

As we noted in chapter 2, if you don't know where you're going, it is usually impossible to get there. A newsroom-learning program must begin with the goals. When news executives have not clearly articulated a manageable number of goals or if they are unwilling or unable to keep the list intact while the learning is going on, it will undermine the effectiveness of a training program—no matter how great the resources devoted to it.

These goals will form the foundation of the learning pyramid: what we are all working on together right now and for much of the group training. The goals also factor heavily in decisions and priorities when it comes to training for individuals in the upper tier of the pyramid.

As we described in chapter 2, newsroom executives at *The Atlanta Journal-Constitution* focused on three goals: more beat watchdog reporting, more use of alternative story forms, and improved community connections. Three may be the most any newsroom wants to take on at any one time. In our experience, newsrooms that limited the number of goals and communicated them vigorously until the learning was deeply absorbed and could be seen in the content were more successful than newsrooms where the goals list kept growing and the focus and training did not keep pace.

An even more modest number of goals may be appropriate. A smaller newspaper, the *La Crosse Tribune,* wanted to focus its first-year training efforts in two areas: cutting back on the length and frequency of turn-of-the-screw local government stories and learning more about local demographics in order to create at least one new print product.

## Put Someone in Charge

Editors who have developed successful newsroom training programs say it is essential to have a staff training coordinator, even if not for a full-time position.

"The key thing we did was to make somebody responsible for it," says Bob Zaltsberg, editor of the *Herald-Times* in Bloomington, Ind. "In a newsroom that has 29,000 circulation, that isn't necessarily the easiest thing to do. But it's one of the best decisions I've ever made."

Zaltsberg, whose Learning Newsroom project committee recommended that every staff member be required to devote at least 12 hours per year to training, says the newsroom is holding a training session every two weeks thanks to having a five-hours-a-week training coordinator.

The key is that someone comes to work every day with training at the top of his list of priorities. That, Zaltsberg and other editors say, may be more important than the number of hours staffers spend per day on the job, especially in smaller newsrooms.

Even in the five hours a week he spends in the newsroom, training coordinator Rod Spaw is highly effective at what he does. "He's come up with really creative ways to train people, going online and finding training opportunities, like having a high News University (Poynter Institute's online training program) presence," Zaltsberg says. "We're accomplishing a huge amount with a pretty small commitment."

In larger newsrooms, the commitment of time devoted to such a project by a training editor may need to be higher. In anticipation of intensifying its training efforts in 2004 and 2005, *The Atlanta Journal-Constitution* shifted from a training editor shared half-time with corporate parent Cox Newspapers to an editor who devoted four days a week to training. In 2006, *Atlanta* gave the training editor a half-time assistant to help manage a robust training operation. *AJC* staff members participated in nearly 12,000 hours of training in 2005, and Garland, the training director, wanted to spend more time creating and improving the in-house curriculum.

Putting someone in charge of training does not mean newsroom leadership shunts this duty aside, checking it off a list of tasks and moving on to the next initiative. Top newsroom editors need to participate and lead training sessions as well as promote them and seize every opportunity to link successful efforts to goals and training.

### Engage the Staff

A staff committee that helps link newsroom goals to training needs and even develops parts of the curriculum can be a creative spark. It can be a messenger that explains goals to staff and brings staff feedback to senior editors. It can be the workhorse that will help pull together a comprehensive newsroom-training program.

The success of *The Atlanta Journal-Constitution*'s training program, which within a year had begun to improve newsroom culture and news content measurably, was rooted in the newspaper's commitment to put many training decisions in the hands of staff. The newsroom leadership did its part in defining the goals and sticking with them, and a lively and engaged staff committee involved its peers in figuring out what success on the goals might look like and what people needed to learn to meet them.

The process provides a strong model for staff engagement through committee work, which we believe is essential to creating training that improves both content and culture.

Whether the goal is culture change or skills-oriented training, engaging staff in the committee to determine what training is needed and to develop the curriculum is key. Adult learners want to learn what adult learners want to learn. If journalists feel they have created something, they are more likely to participate than if they feel something is being imposed on them.

AJC training director Garland says she recruited about a dozen people—mostly staff from various disciplines with a couple of managers—who had "a lot of energy, some creativity and also a sociability factor within the newsroom," qualities that as much or even more than considerable journalistic skill would prove key to success.

The first job of the committee was to understand the top goals and report from their peers in the newsroom what the staff needed to learn to accomplish the goals.

The members of the training committee began conversations with their newsroom colleagues to answer the question: "If you could have any type of training you want, what would it be?"

"It was pretty intense the first couple of months as we discussed what kind of learning atmosphere we wanted at the paper," says Garland. "We interviewed more than a couple of dozen staffers from across the newsroom about what we had done in the past, what would inspire them to learn more, what had worked."

Those conversations brought forth several fresh ideas that might otherwise have gone undiscovered. One of many key lessons from *Atlanta*'s committee is offered by reporter Ty Tagami:

> What they wanted was functional writing and reporting, not doing long two-month pieces, but doing your two-day and one-day stories a lot better. If people were going to train them, they wanted trainers who are known for turning around good stories on deadline, because that's what most people do. They didn't want pie in the sky.

### Illustrate Specific Goals

Even specific goals can be interpreted in different ways. It is important to create models that show what successful achievement of the goal looks like. Staff members can play a key role in doing that. This is a learning experience in itself, one that improves collaboration and communication. As Garland noted, committee work yielded the tag of "ASFs" that everyone in the *AJC* newsroom now uses to say "alternative story forms."

And the specificity goes beyond that. In *Atlanta* and other newsrooms, committee members actually created visual guides to what alternative story forms they were after. The efforts drew heavily on staff expertise. In *Atlanta*, reporter Mark Davis posed the question: "What are the standards for good storytelling on which all can agree?"

Davis found answers in his own newsroom:

> I think a lot of newspapers make the mistake of thinking all the talent is somewhere else. They fail to look within their own ranks to find reporters the rest of the staff can emulate.
>
> We highlighted a select group of colleagues to interview about how to do different stories: profiles, explanatory stories, etc. We asked a standard set of questions: What do you look for? Is there a telling moment in a story that defines the direction of the story? When have you reported enough? When have you not reported enough? Do you know when the story is done?

What emerged are what Davis called "some bare minimums to which all people can ascribe," as well as techniques and tip sheets for more sophisticated storytelling.

### Know the Newsroom, Know the Market

If the training goals are the destination, then pretraining assessment is the point of departure. With your goals in mind, ask where the work stands in a given area. Just as your goals for training need to be specific ("better writing" is not an actionable step but "more frequent use of telling detail" or "more variety of story forms" are), you need to make a specific assessment of where you are on the goal before you start training.

"Our writing is flat" is not specific enough.

"We miss opportunities to make our daily stories more engaging by using narrative techniques" is specific enough to start with (and later discussions will illustrate what is meant by narrative techniques!).

The *La Crosse Tribune* had a simple but effective goal: fewer long, turn-of-the-screw meeting stories, a challenge for a highly local, small newspaper. A review of these types of stories set the stage for the staff to develop a graphic called NewsTracker, which reports routine government actions in brief. The new format, coupled with training on writing, created more tightly produced results.

The *Tribune* saw a significant reduction in the total number of local longer government meeting stories published and significant use of NewsTracker as an at-a-glance replacement for some routine meeting stories.

Counting stories evokes visions of content audits, which can be enormous tasks that produce too much information to be valuable in the run-and-gun atmosphere of the newsroom. But spot counts can give a general picture of where you are and, down the road, whether you're making progress.

In the Tomorrow's Workforce project, we performed more detailed assessments for newsrooms to help them link training needs to culture, market challenges, goals and leadership development needs and produced a report called a "Learning Matrix."

We used a format that examined, in sequence:

- What we saw; an observation about the newsroom.

- The implications of that observation on context of larger goals.

- What learning needs it suggested.

- What result the learning might produce.

We applied the matrix to different areas such as leadership capacity, staff capacity, market demographics and challenges, newsroom resources and readership goals. This helped partner newsrooms see their training needs and challenges in larger context and reinforced the idea that training needs to be linked to solving problems and creating change.

## Identify Trainers and Develop Modules

There are three major sources of teachers who can conduct training in your newsroom:

- Look for staff members who have the expertise you need and help them grow as trainers.

- Hire staff with training skills.

- Bring in outside trainers.

When the *Waco Tribune-Herald* identified continuous development for midlevel editors as a key training priority, it had no money to bring in a trainer on an ongoing basis. It did have, in Managing Editor Becky Gregory, an accomplished editor and coach who was unsure of her teaching skills. So the newspaper sent Gregory to a "train the trainer" workshop at the American Press Institute to boost her teaching ability.

*Atlanta* developed an entire curriculum focused on improving "beat watchdog" reporting led by Jim Walls, an *AJC* investigative editor.

Smaller newspapers may not have the investigative bench to provide extensive watchdog training, but they may develop other experts—in-house writing coaches such as *The Dothan Eagle*'s editorial page editor, Bill Perkins.

Another strategy: add training experience to the qualifications list for key hires. The *Star Tribune* in Minneapolis, eager to increase its computer-assisted reporting efforts, hired IRE trainer Ron Nixon. *Atlanta* looked for writing coach experience and found it in Deputy Managing Editor Shawn McIntosh.

Once you have drawn as much expertise as you can from the staff, think about outside trainers who can fill your highest priority needs. In addition to recommendations from others,[6] make sure your trainers:

- Understand and embrace your goals and are willing to tailor their training to your newsroom needs.

- Follow recent newspaper and online readership research and incorporate its findings and suggestions into the training.

- Can teach in a range of settings—from large groups to smaller discussions to one-on-ones depending on your needs.

- Understand fundamental concepts of adult learning.

Keep in mind basic principles of adult learning: adults learn by doing. Figure 4-3 shows the breakdown of learning practices for adults. It is not our purpose to examine these in detail. There are many resources available and some are listed in the bibliography at the back of this book. This fundament, however, is worth noting.

So it is important that classes include exercises that allow participants to practice skills. That should be a minimum requirement of any skills training session. Even better, the classes should include opportunities to actually do something in real time. *Atlanta*'s beat watchdog training provides one example: participants are sent off on an online scavenger hunt for data and documents; in some cases, a training exercise produced a news story.

### Clarify Expectations for Attendance and Participation

An important question for any newsroom-training program is whether training should be required or merely optional. We believe it is critical that a significant

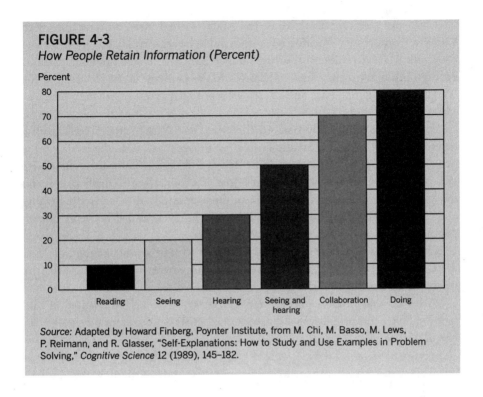

**FIGURE 4-3**
*How People Retain Information (Percent)*

Percent

*Source:* Adapted by Howard Finberg, Poynter Institute, from M. Chi, M. Basso, M. Lews, P. Reimann, and R. Glasser, "Self-Explanations: How to Study and Use Examples in Problem Solving," *Cognitive Science* 12 (1989), 145–182.

amount of training be required, whether it's particular classes, a minimum number of hours of training or a combination of both.

We found that even in newsrooms that devoted substantial resources to training, sessions often were sparsely attended. Most of the staff members who did take advantage were dedicated repeaters with supervisors who valued training. As a result, significant resources—the time and dollar expense of offering the training—were not fully effective and key messages of the training were not widely shared.

A key to successful training is to make sure every staff member understands the goals and their personal roles in moving toward goals and making desired changes. If some staffers—probably those who do not want to change—opt out, it is unlikely the program will create the communications and atmosphere necessary to improve newsroom culture and news content. Thus it also is vital that managers be accountable for the attendance of their staffs.

Finally, making training mandatory sends a message: learning is valued, it's important.

And it's continuous.

That was the message Carlos Sanchez, the editor of the *Waco Tribune-Herald,* was sending when he set a very modest requirement for his 45-person newsroom: five hours training per year.

Based on staff feedback that the staff wanted more interaction with Sanchez, Tomorrow's Workforce recommended he start by leading a brown bag program. With virtually no training budget, Sanchez started biweekly sessions on topics ranging from ethics to changes in the news industry. He scoured the Web for training materials and asked newsroom department heads to lead sessions as well.

Sanchez says he quickly noticed that virtually all the same people from a newsroom staff of about 50 showed up every week and virtually all the same people were absent. That was when he decided to require some attendance. He says it improved the mix significantly: "Just as a football team drills day in and day out during the season, a newsroom must be exposed to constant drilling and training, if it wishes to remain nimble as a business and effective as a newspaper."

Sanchez has this advice for editors who want to start a similar program: "Just do it. Call a brown bag and tell them about your career. Bring the publisher in. Bring the ad director in. Just start."

With even that small requirement, Sanchez says, training has resulted in content improvements and driven the newsroom's shift to more focus on the *Tribune-Herald* Web site.

In other newsrooms, the idea of minimum training hours came from a staff that was frustrated with what they saw as uneven distribution of training. Says Tagami:

> People were having a hard time getting to some of the training we had previously, so someone floated the idea of having a mandatory curriculum, like a college-based curriculum, with credit hours. Making it mandatory and part of your review so everybody knows you've got to go to this and your editor has to give you the time.

*Atlanta* editor Julia Wallace agreed, and the *AJC* adopted a 20-hour minimum per year for staff members and, recognizing the critical role of managers in extending learning into the newsroom, 30 hours for all managers. (Wallace herself would participate in 36 hours of training in 2005.)

In the first year, 2005, *AJC* offered a total of nearly 12,000 hours of training, an average of 25 hours for each of its 485 journalists. Ninety percent of the newsroom staff made the minimums.

Asked somewhat facetiously how the newsroom had increased and improved its print and online content with so many people spending so much time in training, Wallace responded that she thought *AJC* would actually raise the minimum in increments, possibly going as high as 80 hours a year per employee. "Why not 80 hours?" Wallace asks. "People take two weeks of vacation, don't they?"

Table 4-2 shows a sampling of newsrooms that require a minimum number of hours.

**TABLE 4-2**
*Newsrooms Requiring a Minimum Number of Staff and Manager Hours*

| Newspaper (daily circulation) | Staff minimum hours | Manager minimum hours |
|---|---|---|
| The Atlanta Journal-Constitution (350,000) | 20.0 | 30.0 |
| Raleigh News & Observer (165,500) | 15.0 | 22.5 |
| Bloomington Herald-Times (29,000) | 12.0 | 12.0 |
| Corpus Christi Caller-Times (52,000) | 12.0 | 12.0 |
| Waco Tribune-Herald (38,000) | 5.0 | 5.0 |

### Create a Long-range Training Calendar

Figuring out a training calendar takes more than setting some key dates. It must reflect the newsroom's capacity to develop or recruit quality training and have staff attend it. It needs to be frequent enough to support the message that learning is now continuous.

But formal training should not happen so often that the staff gets on overload—straining to get to training and not having time to apply it before the next training sessions are scheduled.

*Atlanta,* with its large staff and mandatory training hours, started 2005 thinking it would offer 40 to 50 sessions during the year. In the end, *AJC* scheduled about 100 classes in 2005—nearly two per week on average—in support of its goal of having every staff member participate in at least 20 hours. The smaller *Waco Tribune-Herald,* after trying weekly sessions, has found a good rhythm in a training brown bag every other week.

*Atlanta* put its schedule—as far as a year out with room for updates and changes—on the newsroom intranet. A good old-fashioned schedule on the bulletin board with e-mail promotions and reminders will work just as well.

Letting people—and their supervisors—plan ahead is critical. Help staff members pick the sessions that are most relevant and interesting to them rather than thumbs up or down on a random session at the last minute.

### Consider Quality of Training

Consider four points of measurement to evaluate training: Did participants find the training useful? Did they learn anything? Did they apply what they learned? How did the application change their performance or what they produced? We believe time-starved newsrooms can learn what they need to know by focusing on the first—reaction—and the last—impact on news content.

For the first, routinely ask whether participants enjoyed the training and whether they are likely to use it in their work.

*Atlanta* asks five questions about classes in its newsroom Cox Academy (named for corporate owner Cox Newspapers):

1. How effective were the instructors on a scale of 1 to 5?

2. If you could suggest one thing to improve the session, what would it be?

3. How would you rank this session on a scale of 1 to 5?

4. What one thing will you take away from this session to use in your job?

5. Please suggest a session you would like to see offered by Cox Academy.

It's a good idea to sample feedback in person as well, interviewing participants individually or in groups. This provides details and undercurrents that training organizers and newsroom leaders may not get on follow-up questionnaire forms. These face-to-face follow-ups may be best conducted by members of the newsroom training committee, who are most likely to get candid comments from their peers. The feedback helps instructors improve and helps the training coordinator and newsroom executives monitor quality.

## Measure Impact of Training

The other essential measurement—one that is typically omitted in the news industry—is measuring whether the training is helping improve the content.

Having training that participants find engaging and relevant is only a first step. What did they actually learn? What learning did they actually use? How did it change the newspaper or online report? And, if not much happened, does the curriculum or the context for learning need adjustment?

As we noted in chapter 2, journalism's measurement system, highly focused as it is on awards from peers, often leaves out day-to-day evidence of impact on content. And if a key purpose of training is change—to improve the journalism in ways that attract and keep audiences—then newsrooms need to apply measures to track that.

In addition to measuring culture change in partner newsrooms, Tomorrow's Workforce evaluated whether the content had actually changed in ways that reflected the training goals. Usually, a simple count of stories, photos or other elements in a 28-day sample of the newspaper told the story.

*Atlanta*'s three pillars of more alternative story forms, more beat watchdog stories and better community connections provide examples.

**TABLE 4-3**
The Atlanta Journal-Constititution's *Use of Alternative Story Forms,*
*2004–2006 (Percent)*

| Story form | Page One | | Local | |
|---|---|---|---|---|
| | 2004 | 2005–6 | 2004 | 2005–6 |
| Traditional | 67 | 43 | 65 | 45 |
| Alternative, visual | 33 | 57 | 35 | 55 |

## ALTERNATIVE STORY FORMS

The paper's goal was less reliance on the inverted pyramid style. We counted stories that used the traditional style and those that used alternative framing, art or display. The results are shown in Table 4-3.

Given *AJC*'s strong shift, we wanted to see whether the story-forms goal was accompanied by any shift in the amount of institution-dominated coverage. Apparently it did, with fewer institution-focused stories and more people and trend stories. The results are shown in Table 4-4.

## BEAT WATCHDOG

*Atlanta's* goal was more short-turnaround enterprise based on public records on local government beats. Through a database library search for stories that had the phrase "public records" in the first three paragraphs, *AJC* found that the number more than doubled, from 40 in 2004 to 95 in 2005.

**TABLE 4-4**
The Atlanta Journal-Constitution's *Shift in Story Topics, from Institutions to*
*People, 2004–2006 (Percent)*

| Story topics | Page One | | Local | |
|---|---|---|---|---|
| | 2004 | 2005–6 | 2004 | 2005–6 |
| Institution-focused | 44 | 35 | 66 | 45 |
| Crime/disaster | 16 | 11 | 16 | 21 |
| People/trends | 15 | 38 | 16 | 33 |
| Sports | 11 | 11 | N/A | N/A |
| Other (including Iraq war) | 14 | 5 | 2 | 1 |

COMMUNITY CONNECTIONS

The newsroom was less aggressive in its community connections pillar, with racial and gender diversity (as measured in photos), increasing only in Living, Metro and Sports.

Wallace says she believes the beat watchdog and storytelling pillars produced better results because the goals were specific and concrete. The community connections pillar was more amorphous and will need more honing to ensure progress. "The clearer the pillar, the better the success," Wallace says.

Obviously, story counts do not provide a complete picture—the quality of efforts must be assessed as the staff experiments, learns and changes over time. But the numbers give a sense of direction and an indication of whether the effort is working or needs adjustment.

Early in 2006, Garland worked with staff members to refine the goal of "community connection." The result was the creation of a "reader immersion" program that takes staff members to different Atlanta-area communities where they report and produce visual galleries to share with others online.

All of this is hard work. In our Tomorrow's Workforce partnerships, we identified three major pitfalls:

- Letting the goals slip away. A few staff committees, flush with enthusiasm and ideas, lined up varied and multiple training opportunities but lost sight of the core goals, diffusing the impact of the training on news content. One committee concluded after one year that it needed to move away from the "buffet" approach to something more strategic.

- Day-to-day practices that fail to reinforce or even undermine the training. If training your frontline editors to coach more effectively might also mean teaching time management, look at whether some routine (but not particularly productive) activities or meetings can be cut back—at least temporarily. One newsroom provided significant training to midlevel editors by emphasizing the need to spend more time coaching reporters; then it scheduled additional weekly meetings with the goal of improved planning. Both were good ideas, but the timing left the managers rolling their eyes and talking about mixed messages; they felt overloaded. Focus on what is important in learning and practicing new skills; let one set of skills sink in before embarking on something different.

- Failure to get buy-in from frontline editors and other midlevel managers. Support for and participation in training is important. And frontline editors—the assistant city or sports or business editors or graphics and photo directors who touch staff and content every day—play a critical role in developing a learning newsroom. We will look at the changing roles, challenges and training needs of these editors in the next chapter.

## CHAPTER 5

# Frontline Editors: Guardians of the Culture

*They talk on a daily basis to the reporters. It's easy to pass along your
thoughts and your feelings about change, for it or against it. I think they are
very influential.*

—Mae Cheng, regional editor of *Newsday*,
president of Unity Journalists of Color

**F**rontline editors can make or break a newsroom. Who hasn't heard the story
of the enthusiastic journalist who comes back from a seminar ready to try
new things, only to see his editor slam the door in his face? Who hasn't heard a
journalist say a frontline editor changed her career by coaching her through
rough spots and being an advocate for her best work?

The primary job of the frontline editor—which encompasses job titles including assignment editor, team leader, graphics or photo editor, and assistant city editor—is to manage the newsgathering staff and to plan and edit news content. This
editor touches virtually everything and everyone in the newsroom, and that touch
can push change forward or hold it back.

More than anyone else, these editors translate their understanding of a newsroom's mission into its daily work. They can foster honest give-and-take. They can
open the door to culture change and creative risk. They can be evangelists for staff
development to drive newsroom goals into the news itself, into both print and
online. Or not.

Few of the more than 100 frontline editors we interviewed highlighted the roles
listed above. Instead, they talked about daily struggles to "put out fires" and to
"wear many hats" (serving bosses, reporters, readers, visual artists, online staff).
They complained of hectic days with little time to talk with their journalists and

even less to reflect. They have problems managing up, down and across. They get no respect.

Said one reporter: "Middle managers get the hell beat out of them."

When newsroom executives overlook the lament of the frontline editor they overlook a strong potential ally in the drive to change. Neglected, a frontline editor is apt to be a naysayer and nitpicker, guardian of the status quo, an obstacle to change. But a little preparation can go a long way with the folks who must simultaneously learn new things and continue to produce multiple daily news reports. Leaders have an opportunity to create an environment in which frontline editors can labor with energy and optimism and transfuse these values to the staff in the daily interactions that shape not only the news product but the newsroom culture.

This chapter will describe the frontline editor job and how it has expanded radically in the last decade. It also will examine findings of the Frontline Editor Project, the coalition of journalists and journalism educators that identified key qualities of a successful frontline editor and found the job requires an extraordinary range of skills.

## THE FRONTLINE ROLE: TAKE A SPIN

It is important to understand how much the frontline job has changed in the last decade. Here is how Jacqui Banaszynski, Knight Chair in Editing at the University of Missouri, describes the frontline editor:

> Draw a circle. In the middle, jot down a title: Assigning editor. Frontline editor. Team leader. Whatever you call the folks in your newsroom who work most closely directing staff and stories.
>
> Now draw a series of lines radiating from the circle, like spokes on a wheel. And on each of those lines, note one of the roles an assigning editor plays, or one of the jobs she must attend to, every day to keep that staff productive and those stories publishable.
>
> Finally, give that wheel a hard spin. Picture it as a Ferris wheel, with each job seated in its own car. As it spins, some jobs rise to the top for a moment as others fade to the background. One gets handed off but a new one climbs on. Just when a task seems dealt with, it comes around again, demanding attention.
>
> Dizzy yet?
>
> Journalists who step into the role of frontline assigning editor—often from the ranks of reporter or copy desk, photographer or graphic artist—find themselves stepping into a dizzying world of multiple responsibilities where all demands seem equal. The first weeks and months on the job can cause a sort of professional vertigo; working journalists who have spent years honing their craft suddenly find themselves teacher and disciplinarian, den mother and shrink, coach and cheerleader.[1]

Banaszynski is dead on. The frontline editor is the hub, the one who embraces or kills ideas, the person who is all at once a coach, an assembly line, a complaint department, an air traffic controller and an editor.

Most of the jobs on Banaszynski's Ferris wheel are new ones. Long gone are the days when frontline editors answered to one boss and simply collected stories from reporters and passed them on. Ask Mae Cheng of *Newsday*, who moved from reporting to frontline editing three years ago. She says it's "a lot more hectic" now than when she started:

> There are a lot more demands. Discussions about how to make news relevant tomorrow when it's all over TV and radio today. You're talking about photo, graphics, visual elements; you're talking about Web feeds, discussions about what goes on the Web now and what can be held for (the newspaper) tomorrow. The range of discussions is a whole lot different than it used to be. Then it was talking to reporters. Now there's a whole series of discussions added on top of that, especially for newspapers trying to figure out who we are in today's environment. That's something top editors are thinking about, and frontline editors are involved in that thought process. It just becomes more complex. And also there's a greater administrative responsibility. We're trying to take a more comprehensive view of the people who work in the newsroom. Now we want to evaluate people and talk about their career goals. Good stuff, important stuff. But it adds to your responsibility if you want to do it right.

At metropolitan daily newspapers, the changes have come in waves:

- *A more diverse workforce in a more professional newsroom.* Out with smoking, drinking and barking. In with human resources departments.

- *The rise of visuals.* From black-and-white photos to color, to complex informational graphics. These require more planning, collaboration and time.

- *More direct contact with readers.* A job that was once reserved for top editors is now shared with everyone.

- *Increased emphasis on readership strategies and (often) decreasing resources used to accomplish them.* Today, the frontline editor not only participates in creating new journalistic products; she often must find a way to create them without additional resources.

- *The 24-hour appetite for online news.* Gone are the days of daylong reporting and weekend reporting for the morning newspaper.

Today, multiplatform publishing offers the news industry a great opportunity. But in the transition, it also is the new 800-pound gorilla in the newsroom. Monica Markel, president of the Society of Metro Editors and deputy metro editor at the *San Antonio Express-News*, relates her latest routine chore: "We have to put a special tag on every story longer than 70 lines, a suggested headline, a suggested summary, three links not related to newspaper content." That may not sound like much, but it can take 10 minutes per story. If you handle six of those stories a day, that's an hour of work.

"Frontline editors tend to be the functional dumping ground of the newsrooms," says Markel. "The upper-level figures they've delegated. Lower down, people think, 'Oh, editors do that.'"

It may be true that nearly everyone in a daily newspaper newsroom is doing more with less these days, and learning new online skills in the process. But nowhere in newsrooms could we find people who were expected to do so much with so little preparation. And we found, of all who work in newsrooms, the reaction of frontline editors to the value of training and the need for newsroom change had the greatest influence on those of their colleagues.

## DEFINING THE ROLE

The Frontline Editor Project conducted a series of six conferences around the United States in 2005–2006, with participation of more than 60 frontline editors as well as journalism educators and news executives. The goal was to systematically study, with the help of a job-profiling expert, the skills required of effective frontline editors and use that understanding to design training for them.

The result was a Frontline Editor Development Profile, an inventory of 23 key skills ranked as "essential," "important" or "relevant." Among other things, the frontline editor must at once be a seller, a thinker, a partner, a coach, an administrator and a leader.

"It's an unusually broad range," says Les Krieger, a psychologist and job-profiling consultant who advised the frontline project. Of the jobs he profiles, the skill list of a frontline editor is "unusually long," which indicates "someone in the middle of somewhat competing priorities."

Essential skills of the frontline editor are:

1. *Evaluative.* This person must be able to think critically. This comes into play in news judgment and editing—assessing information carefully, looking for potential limitations and inaccuracies, finding holes in stories or elements that are out of proportion. It also applies in people management—evaluating ongoing work and performance.

2. *Persuasive.* She has to be able to sell ideas to others. The frontline editor role is one with lots of responsibility and little direct authority. The ability to engender enthusiasm is crucial.

3. *Self-confident.* The frontline editor is called upon to perform in a variety of settings—with peers, with his staff, with the public, with marketing and advertising representatives. A higher comfort level tends to put others at ease.

4. *Collaborative.* Much of the frontline job requires working with fellow editors, down and up. Being collaborative is key to improving newsroom culture.

5. *Curious.* She should be interested in what makes people tick. The ability to understand why people behave the way they do and what they are after is key to motivating people.

6. *Innovative.* Increasingly, the frontline editor is a source of fresh ideas, as well as the person who must encourage and enable creative risk in the newsroom.

7. *Optimistic.* Times are tough. The best frontline editors have a positive—yet realistic—attitude that will rub off on others.

8. *Trusting.* An effective frontline editor is prepared to believe others are reliable and honest but is neither naive enough to be easily taken in—by staff or by stories—or distrusting enough to always expect the worst of people.

9. *Caring.* As a people manager, the frontline editor needs to be sympathetic and considerate of others, but not to the point of being overly drawn into them and making unreasonable allowances.

10. *Fact-based.* To be effective, the frontline editor must be comfortable dealing with data but also be able to operate without quantifiable data. Too far on either end of the spectrum, the editor is apt either to avoid figures and numbers, undermining the journalism, or be a math whiz who is uncomfortable when hard data are not part of the story.

Krieger notes that many of the essential skills in the profile were not management skills but sales skills: being persuasive; knowing what makes people tick; being self-confident, evaluative, collaborative and innovative; and having good command of facts. "They're trying to exert influence in some indirect ways," he says. "Pitching a story. If that isn't selling, I don't know what it is."

Management and administration skills are nonetheless part of the frontline role, reflected in the "important" and "relevant" tiers. Krieger says the effective frontline editor must be:

11. *Achievement-oriented.* The editor sets high personal goals and is prepared to work long and hard in pursuit of excellence. At the same time, this editor cannot be so driven that he loses sight of the need to balance work and life.

12. *Detail-conscious.* The frontline editor must be organized and concerned with detail—checking stories thoroughly for mistakes, for example—but not to the point of losing the big picture.

13. *Rule-conscious.* She must support following rules and procedures but be willing to break them or take a nonstandard approach if the situation warrants it.

14. *Forward-thinking.* The effective frontline editor needs the capacity to develop planning and organizing skills while being comfortable working primarily in changing, often hectic situations.

15. *Affiliative.* Ideally, the frontline editor enjoys being with other people; however, he must balance his time with others with the need to work on his own.

16. *Willing to take charge.* If a group needs a leader, the frontline editor likely will want to fill that role, taking responsibility for organizing the work of others.

At this point, it seems the list contains contradictory, or at least competing, skills. Being a take-charge person and a collaborative one. Following the rules and being willing to break them. Thinking critically and caring.

The next tier features similar nuances. Almost every skill has a caveat—"to a certain extent." The editor must be:

17. *Candid.* The effective editor balances directness and tact, and rarely seeks confrontation but is willing to engage in it in some situations.

18. *Independent-minded.* Another balancing act: The editor must achieve a balance between doing things his way and accepting the need for consensus or a team approach.

19. *Modest.* In a similar vein, the effective editor discusses her achievements and successes but is careful not to overemphasize them at the expense of team accomplishments.

20. *Consistent.* The editor is generally consistent, varying behavior only when it is important to do so and within fairly limited boundaries.

21. *Tough-minded.* The effective frontline editor is not easily offended and can take criticism with a cool head even though doing so may hurt slightly.

22. *Emotionally controlled.* The effective editor usually appears balanced and mature in expressing emotions, being neither too open nor very restrained in expressing feelings.

23. *Self-aware.* This is an ability to understand how his manner and actions affect others, and an honest awareness of his strengths and weaknesses.

Krieger's reaction to the frontline editor profile: "My heavens! Look at all the complexity this individual deals with through the day and all the attributes that are required and the savvy it takes to decide what to use when."

One thing is normal about the job. The typical workplace pattern holds that the mid-level jobs are actually more complex than the top management jobs. "The range tends to go up as you move up the organizational ladder, then starts to shrink back down," explains Krieger. "At the top, a lot of people are filtering for them. In some ways, the job is easier. They're not paid for more job complexity; they're paid for the impact of the decisions they make, good or bad."

So here it is. Jacqui Banaszynski's Ferris wheel, in this case with 23 seats, professionally dissected and designed, for the first time. Now what? Run for cover? Recommend counseling for everyone involved?

No. The point here is that professional development practices, correctly applied to newsrooms, can help them transform into the 21st-century operations they need to be. In this case, that means being sure that these pivotal editors are sufficient in number and adequately trained and supplied to be able to help—and not resist—newsroom change. Newsroom leaders who understand and improve the situation will find that there is a potentially big payoff.

## THE GROUP "ON THE FENCE"

How can the news industry give these highly challenged and pivotal editors what they need to become agents of constructive change?

First, newsroom executives need to listen to them. Frontline editors are often discouraged, at risk of burning out on their jobs, but seeing no place else to go in the organization.

John Greenman, a journalism professor at the University of Georgia and a former newspaper publisher, describes a series of interviews he conducted on behalf of Tomorrow's Workforce at a mid-sized daily newspaper in 2005:

> An editor who'd been in the job for about 18 months was succinct in her response: "disrespected" from above, she told me, "pitied" from below. When I ran her words by a second editor, I heard that the first editor "took the words right out of my mouth." And a third editor concurred: "Absolutely accurate." In notes I jotted while listening, I wrote, "These frontline editors are not well thought of—by themselves—or by others."[2]

Industrial psychologist Pierre Meyer sees frontline editors as key to newsroom change. "This is the group that is on the fence," he says. "This group can prevent change or endorse change. The working journalist is going to be watching this group to see which way they go."

Frontline editors are the guardians of newsroom culture. "I like the term *guardians*," Meyer says. "In some ways you can say the editor and the managing editor are the leaders of improving culture. But this group is the guardians because they can make it work or not."

Often, Meyer says, frontline editors are first to resist the idea of a more collaborative culture. "They do not want to lose the power they have and they still see it as an issue of power as opposed to involvement."

When the Learning Newsroom project took its culture-change program to newsrooms, Meyer says, midlevel editors emerged as pivotal:

> Some quickly said, "That's fine, we can try that." Some others resisted, even though the people working for them thought it was an intriguing idea. That's typical, and it isn't unique to newspapers. A lot of times when any kind of major change is introduced, it's that group that is most skeptical. They're wondering, "What does this mean for me?" I've seen that in many, many industries but in particular in the news industry.
>
> (Middle managers) are saying, "I worked very hard to get to this point, I paid my dues, I worked for authoritarian leaders, demanding people who just pushed output. Now that I'm there, now that I have an opportunity to affect the newspapers and they say I've got to work with everybody."

Butch Ward, Distinguished Fellow at Poynter and a former *Philadelphia Inquirer* managing editor, gives one of an abundance of examples that illustrates how the frontline editor can influence both culture and content.

Say a local frontline editor learns that General Motors was going to close five plants in the region, Ward offers. "I could call my colleague on the business desk and say, 'You need my help today. Let me send you three reporters.' Or I can follow my own agenda. Are we in this together or am I in it primarily for myself?"

The collaborative approach likely improves the quality of the news report on the plant closings and sends a message to the newsroom that teamwork is valued. The go-it-alone approach reinforces the silos that are characteristic of a more defensive organization.

Ward says the daily pressures of the job make it harder for frontline editors to collaborate even as that becomes a more critical priority for newsrooms. "It's more and more difficult for editors to feel generous with their resources," he says. "It's everything they can do to get done what they think they're supposed to get done every day."

When newsroom leaders are quick to criticize an editor for missing a story but slow to praise them for sharing, Ward says, that can throw frontline editors into survival mode.

Many of the decisions a frontline editor makes are small ones; but over the course of days, weeks and months in the newsrooms, they can number in the thousands.

Each carries a message about creativity, collaboration and risk-taking—or the lack of it. Each carries a message about what will be rewarded—or punished. Together, these decisions shape the culture more than pronouncements from the corner office.

If a demoralized and overbooked frontline editor will crawl into the defensive shell, and an optimistic, organized frontline editor will help the newsroom learn to change, how do you get the latter and not the former? You can't without training.

## WHERE AND HOW MIDDLE MANAGERS CAN HELP

Scholar Quy Nguyen Huy, writing in the *Harvard Business Review,* describes a six-year study of middle managers in times of radical organizational change. The study included interviews with more than 200 middle and senior managers. He finds it not at all true that a middle manager will "stubbornly defend the status quo because he's too unimaginative to dream up anything better—or, worse, someone who sabotages others' attempts to change the organization for the better."[3]

Engaged middle managers, it turns out, contribute to radical change at their companies in four major areas:

> First, middle managers often have value-adding entrepreneurial ideas that they are able and willing to realize—if only they get a hearing. Second, they're far better than most senior executives are at leveraging informal networks at the company that make substantive, lasting change possible. Third, they stay attuned to employees' moods and emotional needs, thereby ensuring that the change initiative's momentum is maintained. And finally, they manage the tension between continuity and change—they keep the organization from falling into extreme inertia, on the one hand, or extreme chaos, on the other.[4]

There's a payoff: "if senior managers dismiss the role that middle managers play . . . they will drastically diminish their chances of realizing radical change," Quy says. "Indeed, middle managers may be the corner-office executives' most effective allies when it's time to make a major change in the business."[5]

All this suggests that frontline editors should get a lot of training. But they don't. They are, in fact, among the least likely to be trained. They often don't leave the office, don't go to conferences, and don't typically have their own professional groups. When others go off for training, frontline editors stay behind to "put out the paper." One survey found that only one in five frontline editors received any training before or during their transition to the desk.[6]

"I thought 'I'm a clean writer so I can edit copy. I know what a good story is and I can do that,'" says *Newsday* regional editor Cheng. But she realized "it was more about the leadership skills than it was about the journalism skills. I didn't have to learn to manage up and sideways as a reporter. It's the thing I'm not sure I expected."

We found near universal desire in newsrooms for more training for midlevel editors. In our newsroom surveys, executives and middle managers identified training for the midlevel group as a high priority. Nonmanagers often said more training for their supervisors was a top priority, often on par with the training staff members said they wanted most for themselves.

Greenman, the Georgia journalism professor, has interviewed and surveyed hundreds of journalists who have participated in NewsTrain since 2004. Working with the Associated Press Managing Editors, NewsTrain has traveled the country, offering training to several thousand frontline editors by bringing it directly to them.

Among other things, Greenman asks the editors to describe "the most significant supervisory or managerial problem" they have encountered. "Their answers are consistent and come in four closely related categories," he says.

1. Lack of managerial authority and related new-in-the-role issues.

2. Giving direction, motivating and communicating expectations to staff.

3. Acting on poor, deteriorating or inappropriate performance—including firing.

4. Confronting more and greater demands with fewer resources.[7]

In recent years, the American Press Institute and Poynter also have developed sessions that focus on frontline editors. NewsTrain's traveling curriculum (www.newstrain.org) offers midlevel editors around the country a mix of craft and management training. Poynter's News University (www.newsu.org) offers free or low-cost online courses that will be of interest to frontline editors, including "Listening," "Get Me Rewrite," and "Visual Literacy." NewsU also is developing an online "job fit tool" based on the Frontline Editor Development Profile.

Not surprisingly, newsrooms that train with the "guardians of newsroom culture" in mind see improvements in newsroom culture—most often in attitude changes that lead to better communication.

Chris Hunt, *The Oregonian* Living editor, explained how feedback and coaching helped her better understand what she needed to do to improve:

- Understanding personality differences, and then being able to forge a better relationship with a peer editor with whom she had not been getting along. "It was almost a scientific reason why we didn't get along. It did force the two of us to confront the issues we had working together," says Hunt. "We actually went out to lunch and both of us worked on it really hard. It's completely changed the tenor of our working relationship."

- Working on her listening skills. "I was called out about being a little dismissive when I didn't think a story would work," remembers Hunt. "It really causes me now to stop and listen. It's good to be cognizant of how people react to you. In that regard, the exercise is very helpful."

Frontline editors who receive good training are likely to become evangelists for it. They work to get more for themselves and for their staffs, another lever for improving culture and performance. Greenman found that more than half of about 300 NewsTrain participants went on to participate in additional training themselves. More than 60 percent said they had become "stronger advocates for training," including these actions:

- Encouraged, pushed, helped direct reporters to apply for training, 30 percent.

- Lobbied senior managers to provide resources for additional training, 30 percent.

- Developed, led training sessions, 26 percent.[8]

Training also directly helps develop frontline editor skills—coaching, motivating and communicating, for example. It also can reveal when frontline editors feel cut off from important newsroom work, such as strategy setting.

The frontline job, being connected to all others, can become an echo chamber for larger organizational issues and problems. If the newsroom does not allow supervisors to hold employees accountable, this will show up most noticeably on the frontline level. If time is being wasted in unfocused meetings, these are the editors who will notice it first and loudest. If strategy is being decided without staff input, theirs are the ideas you may miss the most. Most of all, however, there is the simple question of the number of them. Trying to run an organization with three frontline editors when you should have four is trying to run a car on three wheels. These are the jobs where the rubber meets the road. Of all positions, this is the one where priorities must be discussed and work well organized.

We came to believe that the effectiveness of frontline editors often flows directly from that of newsroom leaders. In the first two chapters, we discussed the importance of clear leadership and disciplined goal setting. These efforts help frontline editors immensely.

Frontline editors are "the ones who have to carry out the change," says Pierre Meyer. As editor "I can sit on my high horse and dictate the change I want. This is why the goals expand from 3 to 15. I can sit here and say, 'Here's a good idea, let's try that out here.' The boss can identify more ideas and opportunities than any staff can carry out."

## CHAPTER 6

# Learning to Change:
# The Business Imperative

*The tumult in the industry has forced everyone to recognize that we need to change to be successful and that there is a need for leaders and employees who are trained to handle that.*

—Gary Pruitt, chair, president and CEO,
The McClatchy Company

**E**verything we've discussed until this point—leadership, goals, culture, middle managers, newsroom learning—is about professional growth. But strategic training is also critical for the business of journalism.

In this chapter, we will show how companies that invest in their people and create environments that support innovation are better able to adapt to changes in their markets. They also have highly satisfied employees and outperform their peers financially. These companies devote money and time to ongoing learning because they see it as critical to their core mission.

No company can survive fundamental change by standing still. The American corporate landscape is littered with the remains of retail, manufacturing and technology firms that failed to adapt to competition, could not—or would not—embrace technological innovation or ignored demographic shifts in their markets.

The newspaper industry faces just such a challenge. It stands at what Newspaper Next, the American Press Institute research project launched in 2005, called a "strategic inflection point—a period of disruptive changes that threaten its current way of doing business with no clear future path." [1]

"The industry's very survival is dependent on its ability to reframe completely the way it does business, and find new ways to attract and keep customers," project researchers said. "Many industries throughout history have reached strategic inflection points; not every industry has weathered them successfully."

Gary Pruitt, CEO of The McClatchy Company, which demonstrated long-term commitment to newspapers by its $4.5 billion purchase of Knight Ridder, puts newspapers' predicament even more bluntly:

> The industry has had it forced on them that there is a critical need for change. And it didn't come easily. They tried to hold on to the old model as long as they could. And you understand why? It was great. It was high profit and it was easy. As (investment consultant) Peter Lynch is quoted as saying, "You always want to invest in a company any idiot can run." For a long time, almost any idiot could run a profitable newspaper. Now the margin for error is less. It's more difficult.

Change will demand new forms of leadership and new skills throughout the newspaper industry, says Pruitt, and that increases the need to spend more on training. Some industry executives are prepared to buy into change, but others are not.

"The tumult in the industry has forced everyone to recognize that we need to change to be successful and that there is a need for leaders and employees who are trained to handle that," says Pruitt. "On the other hand, there's a sort of bunker mentality that may actually rein in any training spending because some people think they have to weather this storm."

Laurie Bassi, CEO of McBassi & Company, a research and human resources management firm, says executives who think they can survive by hunkering down are kidding themselves. "An organization's ability to respond effectively to constant (and inevitable) changes in its environment hinges on its ability to learn," she says. Training and developing employees in challenging times provides the institutional "resiliency" to survive change, says Bassi. "It's like emergency preparedness, having the stuff it's going to take to get you through a crisis of an uncertain origin at an unknown time."

What happens to industries in decline? They "disinvest," Bassi says, and provides an example:

> A classic example is the steel mills in Pittsburgh. They are rusted. They're being depleted. You might say, well, that's what is causing their decline, but it's actually a symptom of their decline, a purposeful disinvestment. It looks to me like that's what's happening in the newspaper industry. They're not planting new seeds, they're harvesting. That strategy will work for a while, but those who emerge as the eventual leaders, or even the survivors, are those who take an alternative approach.

The newspaper industry's disinvestment included the elimination of more than 2,000 newsroom jobs in 2005. Overall, newspaper industry employment fell 18 percent between 1990 and 2004.[2] And because training is routinely seen as a cost rather than as an investment, we found its budget trimmed (or stricken completely) in many newsrooms.

In contrast, research by Bassi's company and others shows[3] that investors value companies that place a priority on employee learning. In a study of 600 companies, Bassi's firm found that "hypothetical portfolios made up of those firms that made the largest investments in employee development had an annualized return of 16.3 percent in the following year, compared with an annualized return of 10.7 percent for the S&P 500 for the same period."[4]

Nationally, corporate spending on training has increased since the last recession. On average, companies spend an estimated 2.3 percent of payroll on it,[5] more than five times as much as the newspaper industry, according to an analysis by the Inland Press Association.

Some news industry leaders resist disinvestment. "My gut reaction is that we're at a transformational stage," says Jay Smith, president of Cox Newspapers. "We're at a point as a business where so much has changed around us, and we really haven't changed with it. If we think we can cut our way to prosperity, we're kidding ourselves."[6]

The Readership Institute at Northwestern University has long linked training and other investments in employee development to business success: "People factors are twice as important as economic factors when explaining the overall differences between high performing companies and average performing companies."[7]

Indeed, a study by consultants Roberts, Nathanson & Wolfson of 5,200 organizations found that "world-class development practices targeted at 'rank and file' individuals throughout the organization make a significant impact on business results."[8] The study also found that strategic training enables organizations to become more constructive and more flexible. Training, the study said, is "learning for their future success."

Mary Nesbitt, managing director of the Readership Institute, says strategic training "institutionalizes the notion that in order to be adaptable, in order to respond to the market, which is what all businesses do, we need to be a continuously learning organization."

Training also tells people what the company thinks is important, Nesbitt says. It's part of the "so that" equation—training so that you can do something. Even more important, a company that invests in its employees tells them they are important, and from that Nesbitt sees a bonus. Not only, she says, does training help "the company realize its stated goal, but it also leads to improvements and innovations that had never been thought of before" because people are "being encouraged and rewarded" for thinking.

A thinking newsroom. What a good idea!

## PEOPLE MAKE THE DIFFERENCE

As newspapers strive to become dynamic competitors in a fierce information economy, good editors know they must find an edge to distinguish their news products from the glut of other media offerings. The skill, energy and motivation of a newsroom staff can be the difference between a newspaper that successfully reinvents itself and one that doesn't. Says Robert Reich, former secretary of labor:

> The truest and simplest argument these days is this: Nowadays, any competitor can get access to the same information technology, the same suppliers, the same distribution channels, and often the same proprietary technology. The only unique asset that a business has for gaining a sustained competitive advantage over rivals is its workforce—the skills and dedication of its employees. There is no other sustainable competitive advantage in the modern, high tech, global economy. Barriers to entry are dropping like mad, so the quality of your workforce in terms of innovation and customer relations is basically all there is.[9]

Companies that train see the training as an asset, not as an expense. They see it as driving a constructive culture, one with an appetite for innovation, which in turn improves the bottom line. "It's something the leaders in the best companies talk about all the time," says Amy Lyman, president of the Great Place to Work Institute, which puts together *Fortune* magazine's "100 Best Companies to Work For" list.

"If you want people to be innovative," Lyman says, "they need to have the smarts and the skills and the knowledge, but they also need to have the freedom, the comfort and the support to try things that are new and may fail."

The chief executives of such companies point to positive cultures supported by strategic learning as a secret of their business success. An example is Northwest Community Hospital in Arlington Heights, Ill. Doctors say it is one of the best facilities in the country. In 2006, it was named to *Fortune*'s "100 Best" list. CEO Bruce Crowther sums up his approach: "I believe culture solidly trumps strategy. Our employees and our desirability as an employer are the foundations of every success that we achieve."[10]

The Great Place to Work Institute says Northwest Community Hospital's "greatest competitive advantage" is a strong workplace culture based on regular training for managers and staff. When the hospital decided to change its culture several years ago, its first step was to form an in-house university that focused initially on managers. Why managers? "Because," one executive said, "to have a great culture, you need managers who understand that employees are at the center of everything we do."[11] Today, the hospital's university offers training for all employees.

Forward-looking executives in the newspaper industry say newspapers need to concentrate on workforce development as part of a long-term survival strategy.

Journalists are newspapers' critical strategic assets. Providing them with new tools for new forms of journalism can enable newspapers to take charge of change and shape their own future.

"Thinking about training and development in business terms—there is no question, no question in my mind at all, that it's essential to our success," says Cox's Jay Smith. "I think it's every bit as important as what we spend on newsprint, what we spend on travel, what we spend on all those line items in a budget. Because if we don't make the commitment to do it what we're saying is that we don't care, that we are prepared to lose ground as the world grows more complex with each passing day, and to lose ground effectively is ultimately to lose."

Most top executives would agree. Nearly seven in 10 global business leaders believe "that retaining talent is far more important than acquiring new blood," found the consultant group Accenture. "People have become the key competitive differentiator in today's knowledge-based economy."[12]

The newspaper industry is not the only one facing reinvention of its basic products and business practices. Everywhere, the Accenture study reported, "issues relating to the workforce have become among the highest strategic priorities on the executive agenda at companies around the world." To be competitive, executives listed four of their top priorities as "attracting and retaining skilled staff; improving workforce performance; changing leadership and management behaviors; and changing organizational culture and employee attitudes."[13]

Hiring and keeping smart people. Doing more. Reinventing leadership. Reviving culture. Training works with each of these priorities—it gives employees more skills, it improves leadership communication and vision and it directly affects culture. But that's not all.

## TRAINING ATTRACTS THE BEST AND HELPS KEEP THEM

Training not only makes employees better at what they do, it helps keep them from walking out the door. With all the challenges newspapers face, they don't need to lose their best people. Yet newsroom turnover increased significantly during the 1990s, reaching 23 percent in 1999 (compared to an all-industry average of 15 percent).[14] It can be higher still in small newsrooms, which serve as stepping-stones for journalists fresh out of college and on their way to larger newspapers.

Losing accomplished or promising employees hurts a business three ways: productivity drops because skills walk out the door; managers (the most expensive employees) become distracted by the hiring process; and morale falls among remaining employees who have to shoulder the extra work and wonder why they are staying when respected, expensive colleagues are leaving.

Turnover is also expensive—very expensive. That is one reason company trainers like to use this quote from management guru Tom Peters: "If you think training is expensive, try ignorance." Let's do some math. A typical business spends about 1 to 2.5 times an employee's salary to make a hire—the price paid for direct costs such as recruiting, interviewing and relocating as well as indirect costs such as managers' time. Take a newspaper with a newsroom staff of 75, an average salary of $40,000 and a 20 percent annual attrition rate. For this newspaper, replacing 15 staff members a year at an average cost of 1.5 times salary each could cost the newspaper up to $900,000 a year.

Keeping just one of those 15 staff members from leaving would save $60,000 in direct and indirect costs. That represents 2 percent of payroll, which is near the average amount spent on training and staff development in all industries (compared to the latest estimates of 0.4 percent for newspapers). Simply put, if newspapers spent even just a little bit more on training, they could save a bundle on hiring.

The connection between lack of training in the newspaper industry and employee dissatisfaction is well documented. In a 1993 study, "No Train, No Gain," The Freedom Forum linked lack of training to quality, morale and retention problems in the industry. In 2002, a Knight Foundation study, "Newsroom Training: Where's the Investment?" found lack of training was the biggest source of newsroom dissatisfaction, even ahead of pay and benefits, and that more than two-thirds of journalists receive no regular training. In 2003, the Newspaper Association of America (NAA) declared that the industry faced a "talent crisis" because it failed to draw the best and brightest graduates from the nation's universities.[15] Those it did attract, especially young journalists of color, it lost to other businesses. Why? The NAA cited lack of "opportunities for personal growth and development" as primary factors.

All in all, the NAA said, employees quit for four primary reasons. Strategic training can directly correct at least three of them:

- *Lack of empowerment.* Training leaders improves their ability to provide clear direction, making it easier for employees to participate in decision making. It also encourages leaders to listen and delegate more, which both foster employee engagement.

- *Lack of career opportunities and growth path.* Training employees gives them skills to enhance their careers. A newsroom-wide strategic learning plan provides a growth plan not just for individuals but for the organization as a whole.

- *Dissatisfaction with managers.* Training managers improves their ability to communicate, enabling them to coach more and plan better.

- *Dissatisfaction with compensation.* Training may not necessarily lead to a pay raise, but having more skills and knowledge about the industry makes a journalist more valuable—to his current employer.

Training won't cut turnover to zero. But it helps. Consultants Roberts, Nathanson & Wolfson found in their survey of 5,200 organizations that those with greater levels of staff development had 57 percent higher retention than otherwise comparable organizations.[16]

A company that invests in its employees also finds it can recruit the best people. Hiring well is a crucial first step for any successful business. The Readership Institute reported that research of almost 1,800 organizations indicates that the "business impact one can expect from selecting and hiring high-caliber talent is truly enormous." The better the talent, the greater the productivity.[17]

Increasingly, though, newspapers are having difficulty attracting the best graduates of the nation's communications schools. With average starting newsroom salaries hovering in the mid-$20,000s—about what a barista makes in a big-city Starbucks—newspapers must offer more than money as a magnet. Experts say creativity, workplace culture and opportunity for professional growth are the biggest draws—characteristics more typically found in nonjournalistic media jobs like advertising or publishing, or, more recently, in online news organizations run by nonnewspaper companies like Google or Yahoo.

The NAA says newspapers are coming up short in hiring. "Newspapers feel they are dealing with a mounting crisis in getting and keeping good people," it claims. "In countless conversations with newspaper executives, two themes recur: 'We've got candidates for jobs, but we don't seem to be getting the cream of the crop anymore,' and 'We keep losing the people we can't afford to lose.'"[18]

The people who do join the newspaper industry, says the NAA, do so

> because the type of job and the nature of the work appeal to them, and because they see opportunities for personal growth and development.... 
> For people still at newspapers, the freedom and autonomy that seemed attractive when joining the newspaper become less so with the passage of time. In addition, current employees express dissatisfaction with other important elements of empowerment such as feeling free to voice one's opinion, and feeling that the newspaper does a good job involving employees in decisions that affect them.... Overall, however, the survey reveals that expectations for growth and development are not being realized. Also included in the development category are lack of training and career advancement opportunities as well as not getting enough feedback and coaching.

The retention strategy of most companies is overly skewed toward money, Accenture found, when studies have shown "that providing employees with a comprehensive range of career and skills-development opportunities is the key to attracting and retaining the kind of flexible, technology-savvy workforce needed to succeed in the digital economy."[19]

Surveys show that high-potential employees—those young people with the drive and the talent to become tomorrow's newsroom leaders—want to be trained and mentored, want to participate in decision making and want to have career opportunities that are not limited by narrow job definitions.

Competition for these young professionals is high in the newspaper industry, as it is in other fields. There are many parallels, for example, between the news business and the legal profession. Both depend on well-educated professionals; both are knowledge industries; both attract driven people; both are highly competitive. But there is no comparison between the salaries major law firms pay to first-year graduates of elite law schools and those of first-year journalists.

Still, many law firms say that what separates them from their competitors—not only in their ability to recruit and retain promising young attorneys, but also in the marketplaces of litigation and negotiation—is their emphasis on training, education and career development.

David Cruickshank, director of professional development and training at Paul, Weiss, Rifkind, Wharton & Garrison, the 500-attorney New York law firm, oversees a staff development program that provides 115 courses a year (most in-house).

The extensive training effort is critical for both recruiting and adapting to a changing legal climate, one whose challenges are very similar to those faced by the newspaper industry—pricing pressures from clients, increasing competition and an incoming workforce whose restlessness outweighs its loyalty to any one employer.

Today's law school graduates are sophisticated, says Cruickshank. "Training is what's going to allow them to develop themselves to move on to the next area. A good percentage of them look at our catalog of courses and listen to the pitch we give them on the training they're going to get and say, 'OK, that makes you different from another place.'"

What about those who fear that their journalists, if trained, would immediately leave? As the development director of another large law firm told us, "We don't worry about that. What are we going to do? Keep them stupid so they'll stay? . . . It's part of the way we do business."

The legal profession, like the newspaper industry, has faced tough challenges economically in recent years. Some firms cut staff development budgets. But at Paul, Weiss and other firms, they found ways to train more economically. They began teaching each other—second-year associates giving classes for first-year grads, senior associates offering career planning, partners leading seminars on management and budgeting. It was good for everyone, says Cruickshank. "Most of them report that they learn a hell of a lot just from going through the process of preparing to teach," he says. "That's an unsung benefit. The leadership, the motivation, the role modeling that happens when faculty get involved, when your peer faculty are involved in teaching. It's a real selling point for continuing education in any profession."

At the beginning of the Tomorrow's Workforce project, we interviewed executives from a diverse range of companies known for investing in their employees. These executives worked in industries ranging from law to pharmaceuticals to high technology. Each delivered the same message: training makes better employees, and better employees make for better business. No one, though, delivered that statement more directly—or memorably—than Jessie McCain, a managing director at TD Industries, a large Texas construction firm and perennial member of the *Fortune* "Best Companies to Work For" list.

Why spend the money on training? we asked. "It depends on why you're in business," was McCain's answer. "If you can do your job and run your company with monkeys, go ahead. We can't."

## TRAINING WORKS: REAL-WORLD RESULTS

Newspapers that are making strategic training a priority are reaping benefits, even in these difficult times. They are seeing significant changes in the content of their news pages and the response of their readers.

*The Atlanta Journal-Constitution,* as we showed in chapter 2, set specific editorial goals for its newsroom and supported them with an ambitious training program. The result: more watchdog stories in the newspaper, more nontraditional storytelling and more engagement by staff in the direction of the paper (and the design of the training).

Says *Journal-Constitution* editor Julia D. Wallace:

> We saw real movement. More than 80 watchdog stories in 2005, everything from a weeklong series on the lack of consumer protection in Georgia to the revelation of a gambling trip of county officials and developers. Alternative story forms appeared in every section, and some brand research showed we made real inroads with suburban readers, who now see us as writing about the entire metro area, not just the city of Atlanta.

*The Oregonian* entered the Tomorrow's Workforce project with a strong record of training. Editors found that by aligning their training with the newspaper goals—that is, making it more strategic—they were able to intensify its impact.

Our interviews identified a need for beat development training that would help reporters develop more enterprise stories, which in turn would attract readers for stories they could not find elsewhere. The newspaper implemented a series of in-house reporting classes that editor Sandy Rowe says have brought more hard-edge stories to the news pages. "Our beat reporting has sharpened reporters' sense of news and ability to mine daily and enterprise stories," she says. "We are, more than ever, holding people and institutions accountable through document-driven reporting. Some of the more accomplished members of the staff have led the way in building and analyzing original databases in such areas as political campaign contributions, school test scores and executive compensation."

The message other top editors can take from *The Oregonian*'s success is simple, Rowe says: "If editors understood how necessary training is to achieve their own goals, they would find ways to make sure it gets accomplished."

A newsroom doesn't need the assets of a large regional newspaper like *The Oregonian* to benefit from training. Consider what has happened at the *Tribune-Herald*, a 38,000-circulation Cox newspaper in Waco, Texas. Editor Carlos Sanchez and Managing Editor Becky Gregory faced the challenges of every small-town editor—too much to do, not enough time or people to get it done.

Sanchez and Gregory wanted more training for their employees, but because the budget was tight they knew they would have to start it themselves. We helped them focus their priorities and form a newsroom training committee, which later took over much of the job of making the brown bag programs happen.

Today, the newsroom has a consistently strong brown bag program every other week. Follow-up newsroom surveys indicate the brown bags and other training programs are improving newsroom culture, which Sanchez believes has powered digital innovation. He says:

> The single most defining moment was having a copy editor, perhaps our biggest cynic of procedural changes, unilaterally declare his own brown bag. We attended and were delighted with a presentation on alternative story forms that not only encapsulated our emerging philosophy, but that he was able to articulate better than we ever had, because he had scoured the country for examples. When he was challenged on a point, he declared, "That's not how we do things anymore." That moment epitomizes what is the most delightful aspect of our training: the moment of buy-in by individual staff members.

A footnote to this story: The brown bag Sanchez mentions was led by a staff member who once told editors that change was not needed "because we have done it this way for 100 years."

Sanchez is a believer. For him, training works. "Just as a football team drills day in and day out during the season," he says, "a newsroom must be exposed to constant drilling and training if it wishes to remain nimble as a business and effective as a newspaper."

Apparently, journalists at the *Tribune-Herald* are believers as well. Turnover at the paper has fallen nearly 40 percent in the last couple of years. Sanchez credits training for the change and says he has heard of staff members recommending the newspaper as a good place to work.

Bob Zaltsberg, editor of the *Herald-Times*, a 29,000-circulation newspaper in Bloomington, Ind., is also a believer. He says his newsroom's engagement with the Learning Newsroom and its training program is having positive impact both inside and outside the newspaper.

The moment that did it for Zaltsberg took place on September 11, 2006.

> I was away at a seminar and when I saw our newspaper the next day I was ecstatic. The front page was art, graphics and breakouts. It was a very good "reader" page, with many interesting things, mostly local and all informative and readable.
>
> I told our managing editor what a great job of planning was done. She said she was minimally involved.
>
> I told our news editor what a great job he'd done on planning. He said he was minimally involved. He said the Sunday night Page One person, who's not a manager, conceived, planned and executed the page in collaboration with her colleagues on the desk. She took the responsibility to make the newspaper the best it could be within the readership goals we've all agreed upon.

That's a constructive culture—when journalists understand their newsroom's goals and feel empowered to act on their best judgment to achieve them.

The *Herald-Times* readers seem to be reacting positively to changes in the paper, says Zaltsberg. Single copy sales are up 10 percent daily and 11 percent Sunday over a year ago, he says. "I believe our Learning Newsroom work has been a significant contributor, in that our knowledge of single copy sales and communication with our circulation department has improved dramatically," he says. "We follow a lot of principles of building readership in our Page One decision making, targeting occasional readers, young readers and people who identify themselves as non-newspaper readers."

More training. More work on turning a defensive culture into a constructive one. More readers. This is the formula forecast by the Readership Institute in its benchmark Impact Study, whose "research shows that newspapers with constructive cultures tend also to have higher readership. The finding echoes results from hundreds of studies in other businesses that link the culture of the workplace to business outcomes."[20]

The lesson from Bloomington is that newspapers can move the readership needle. Training alone won't accomplish that. But it is critical to an integrated strategy that includes progressive leadership, editorial focus, multiple platform publishing, reader engagement and professional development.

The *Tribune* in La Crosse, Wis., is another success story. A year and a half after it partnered with Tomorrow's Workforce, the 32,000-circulation newspaper had a substantial list of accomplishments. It met newsroom content goals, including a big cut in government meeting stories and launch of a weekly section aimed at busy women. It improved the workplace culture among nonmanagers. And it tripled the hours of training available.

"The training plan in some ways really set the tone for the overall goals," says editor John Smalley. "I think by providing to the staff—really for the first time—a clear and directed training plan, there was some added credibility to all of our other efforts."

The *Tribune's* training program is robust and inexpensive, proving again that any good editor with the will to create a training program can find the means. The paper offered an average of 36 hours of training per newsroom professional in 2005, a 525 percent increase over 2004. The cost: about $25,000 in salaries for staff time and $11,340 in direct spending. That is more than one full-time equivalent devoted to training and about 2.5 percent of payroll, more than five times the newspaper industry average and on par with the training average for all U.S. industries.[21] It is also only about $1 per subscriber per year.

## TRAINING WORKS: MAKING DIGITAL REINVENTION REAL

*The Bakersfield Californian*, a 61,000-circulation newspaper in California's Central Valley, is a model for Web-oriented innovation. In 2004, the *Californian* launched *Northwest Voice*, an online-only edition featuring primarily reader-generated content, targeted at a growing section of the Bakersfield community.

In 2005, the *Californian* rolled out Bakotopia, a Web site aimed at the region's young people. Bakotopia is "widely considered to be one of the first U.S. newspaper-backed providers of free classifieds and social networking."[22]

Today, the *Californian* operates with a fully converged newsroom, its 80 staffers moving fluidly and fluently between the print and online publishing worlds. Mike Jenner, its executive editor, says the growth of the newspaper's digital abilities directly paralleled the rise in newsroom training.

The number of training hours at the paper rose more than 70 percent from 2004 to 2006, with a heavy emphasis on multimedia skills. "Not one hour was devoted to multimedia training in 2004," says Jenner. In 2005, "that number was 76 hours; this year we've recorded 276 hours of training in Web video, audio and other convergence issues. This does not include one-on-one training in multimedia editing, which takes place nearly every day."

The titles of the newspaper's training sessions reflect the paper's new digital priorities, says Jenner. "One of the programs we presented was about how to grab readers with headlines on the Web," he says. "Another was how to do a live remote TV interview. Another was how to target audiences in story selection. Another was about rethinking the wire."

The result: "Our overall page views are up," says Jenner. "Our posts and our comments are way up on our blogs. And downloads of our videos are through the stratosphere." Some details:

- One hundred percent of the reporting staff has written an "early take" for the Web on stories headed for print, averaging about nine stories per weekday.

- All reporters use audio and video; 14 of 24 reporters have edited their own video.

- Through mid-November 2006, the staff produced 600 online videos that generated 120,000 downloads. By comparison, in November 2005, they produced six videos.

- The staff publishes 21 blogs and does six regular weekly podcasts.

But, says Jenner, "the area where we succeeded most has been how fully the staff has embraced the Web—how quickly and how universally we've moved. That's where our biggest success has been."

Daily coaching and regular, focused training on technique encourages staff to try new things online, says Jenner.

"We're big believers in short training programs," he says. On Friday mornings, for example, *Californian* staff gather in the newsroom conference room for a 20-minute video-and-cookies program. "Everybody will watch everybody else's video from that week and critique it," says Jenner.

"It has engaged the staff," says Jenner. "It makes the training accessible. It makes the training fun. It's not a burdensome, plodding kind of thing, or not something where you've got to cut out a day or more and leave the building and let all your other work slide into the ditch because you're trying to learn this new thing."

In addition to training in the use of digital journalism tools, Jenner says the *Californian* also emphasizes business literacy. He wants reporters and editors to understand the role the Web will play in the future of newspapers:

> Our staff has a very high level of awareness of what's going on in the journalism world and the newspaper industry. They pay attention to what's happening. There's an awareness out there that the ground is shifting beneath our feet. There's an urgent need for change and we can't run from it. We need to run to it.
>
> The Web is everybody's opportunity, everybody's chance to learn new skills and be more valuable and to create more value that is going to help our readers and help our business.

It would be hard to find a better example of the link between training and editorial innovation than the *Hamilton Spectator* in Ontario, Canada. In 2003, the newspaper underwent a radical reinvention—whole sections killed off, entire new ones added—that led to a rise in readership.

In October 2006, the *Spectator* launched what it called Revolution 2, a remake of the A section that Mary Nesbitt of the Readership Institute described this way: "There's a great blend of long, short and alternative story forms. Carefully selected and powerful visuals. Clear, uncomplicated design. Sharp, unique news decisions that look out for readers' interests."[23]

The *Spectator* took a year and a half to plan its first reinvention. The second took three months. The difference, says editor Dana Robbins, was training:

> Training is like pixie dust. It makes magic happen. It took us 18 months to gear up for the launch of Revolution 1. Revolution 2 we did in less than three. A huge part of that was a function of the training, development and cultural work we did in-between.
>
> Any news organization that believes it can move forward without investing in the development of its staff is kidding itself. In fact, there has probably never been a time when it has been more absolutely crucial to grow the capacity of the people in our newsrooms.

## TRAINING WORKS: CHANGING NEWSROOM CULTURE FOR THE BETTER

Strategic training changes not only the type of work journalists do but the culture of the newsrooms in which they work. As we reported in chapter 3, before-and-after surveys done in the newsrooms that worked with Tomorrow's Workforce or the Learning Newsroom showed culture in most of those newsrooms becoming less defensive and more constructive. Even in newsrooms where overall culture change was lagging, pockets of the staff who had received intensive training showed progress.

Traditional journalism training programs focused on hierarchy, department or task—workshops for managers, reporters or the sports staff. We urged newsrooms to train across departments and across levels—reporters and editors together, midlevel managers from all departments, for example. The results included common understanding of the training and its purpose, shared problem-solving in putting the training into practice and softening of hard department silos. Some staffers even reported the pleasure of meeting colleagues from other departments with whom they had worked for years but never met.

Editor Julia D. Wallace enthusiastically describes the in-house training program's impact on the *Journal-Constitution:* "The difference in how the departments work together and how the newsroom works with other departments has changed pretty dramatically." She attributes the changes to a mix of goal clarity, the training, focusing on key personnel and the way the leaders are reinforcing the message. From training, "you have the vocabulary," she says. "Then it's also the reinforcement. Instead of saying, 'That was a great story,' say, 'That was a great watchdog story.' Instead of saying, 'That was a great living cover,' say, 'That was a great use of an alternative story form.'"

The more journalists collaborate, the more they improve newsroom culture. Instead of finding obstacles to change and improvement, they find solutions and means for innovation. Newsroom surveys in 2004 and 2006 bore that out in Atlanta. The culture of the *Journal-Constitution* newsroom improved during the course of the Tomorrow's Workforce project. Entire departments became more constructive, as did whole tiers of management. Long-term cultural change takes three to five years to gel, so some individuals and some departments remained stuck in their defensive mindset. But the attitude shift seen in just two years showed the newsroom is on its way to becoming an adaptive organization.

At *The Oregonian,* we identified a desire for more leadership training for top editors and team leaders. *The Oregonian* launched a leadership training program that utilized the expertise of Jill Geisler from The Poynter Institute. Three dozen editors participated in the project, which included 360 performance reviews and follow-up discussions.

Executive Editor Peter Bhatia says the training has been "very beneficial. . . . It is sort of like holding a mirror up in front of your face." He has seen changes in team leaders as a result. "They are doing a much better job of leading their teammates," he says. Managing Editor Therese Bottomly notes that the process was "really eye-opening" and that "there were some people who really did take it seriously to change their behavior."

A follow-up newsroom culture survey found that after training these editors were more constructive.

The *Dothan Eagle,* a 31,600-circulation newspaper in Dothan, Ala., committed heavily to training during its engagement with Tomorrow's Workforce and saw quick results. Follow-up surveys two years into the project showed defensive behaviors on the decline and constructive communication and creativity on the rise.

"I would say our employee satisfaction and newsroom culture is at an all-time high," says editor Ken Tuck. "By investing heavily in training for the entire staff, it has shown them that management cares about each person, and we desire to see them reach their fullest potential. Before the training program, we invested a lot more in editors than staffers. Now the training money is spread out more equitably throughout the entire staff. Employees appreciate that.

"Training goes hand-in-hand with improvement," says Tuck. "The more quality training you can provide your staff, the better they become and the better the newspaper and Web site become."

That is a lesson *Caller-Times* editor Libby Averyt learned when the Corpus Christi newspaper broke the story of Vice President Dick Cheney's accidental shooting of a fellow bird hunter in February 2006. We wrote about the 52,000-circulation Texas newspaper in chapter 3 as an example of its newsroom culture change—change Averyt directly ties to training, of herself, her key managers and the newsroom staff. On the Cheney story, Averyt and other newsroom leaders stepped back and watched the staff take the initiative and produce good journalism.

"It has been one of the biggest things we've taken away from the Learning Newsroom," she says. "Before this it was very scattershot. It was sort of expected that if you had your own initiative to get some training that was great. And if you were lucky the paper would pay for it once in a while. It was always part of our evaluation process, but it wasn't something we talked about routinely. It wasn't something that was just part of our daily lives around here."

The Learning Newsroom's training helped the *Caller-Times* take its already committed staff to new levels of communication and collaboration.

"People speak up about issues or problems or opportunities that don't necessarily relate to their individual job," Averyt says. "People aren't afraid to say, 'You know, I think over here we really need to try this.' In the old days somebody may have said, 'You know, that's really none of your business.' And you don't hear that anymore here."

## USING HIGH-QUALITY JOURNALISM TO FOCUS ON THE READER

Many newspapers are committed to excellence and to the training their staffs need to achieve it. Others, though, are content to just get by. And, say some leaders in the industry, this lackadaisical approach to quality is damaging their chance to hang on to old audiences and attract new ones.

"This is what burns me up," says Karen Dunlap, president of The Poynter Institute.

> There's a lot of conversation in the industry about declining audiences and a lot of talk about young people who don't read. There needs to be an equal emphasis on the poor craft quality in many news organizations. They are often guilty of poorly selecting topics, poorly reporting them, and poorly organizing them. And then we say audiences are migrating. I would say a majority of citizens are exposed regularly to very poor journalism. That's something we can change. We could raise the quality of journalism and we need to do it through training.

Being "reader-focused" is a phrase we heard in many newsrooms. Producing the type of high-quality journalism Dunlap would like to see more of requires not just training, but also focus on readers, of both print and online. And that's good for the boardroom as well as the newsroom.

Because training improves the ability of an organization to adapt, it is critical to developing a culture of quality focused on gaining readers. As we have seen from the examples in this chapter—from Atlanta, Portland, Dothan, Bloomington and Corpus Christi—training improves culture, raises the quality of journalism and emboldens journalists to take the initiative on innovation.

A reader-focused news organization "expects continuous innovation in the service of readership," says the Readership Institute. "If innovation isn't made part of the stated expectations for departments and individuals, newspapers will do essentially the same things and get substantially the same results."[24]

Training works. It gets results. And not the same old ones.

## CHAPTER 7

# The Future

*I think it's so clear that if we stand still, our industry really will die. We have to change. We can't expect our employees and our staff to grow and change if we are not willing to invest in them.*

Libby Averyt, editor,
*Corpus Christi Caller-Times*

Journalists need more training. They know it. Their bosses know it. Many corporate leaders also know it. But training, a force that at once accelerates change and eases its difficulty, still is a low priority in the news industry.

In "Investing in the Future of News," a survey funded by the Knight Foundation in 2006, nine in 10 American journalists say they need more training. Nine in 10 newsroom executives agree. The executives also admit they need more training themselves. This hunger to learn crosses multiple topics, from craft skills training, including new media, to ethics and legal affairs to management.

Yet only three in 10 news organizations say they are doing more training today than they did five years ago. Even though every aspect of the news business is changing, at most news organizations midcareer training is stalling or even vanishing. It's as though only a third of America's newsrooms intend to have a future. The good news is that this number is slowly growing; the bad news is that the other end of the bell curve also is growing. Overall, training in the news industry hasn't changed in the five years since Knight funded "Newsroom Training: Where's the Investment?" Then, as now, the No. 1 source of dissatisfaction among working journalists was lack of training.[1]

The Knight survey, released in 2007, was conducted by Princeton Survey Research Associates International, which contacted 2,000 news media journalists

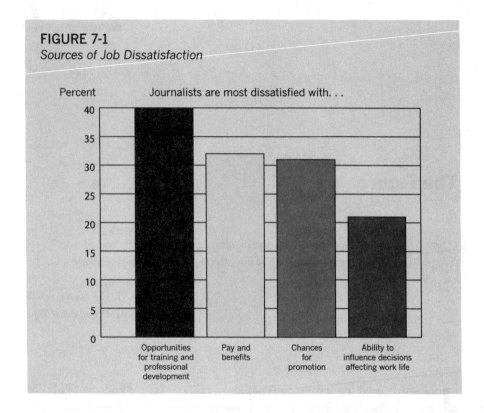

**FIGURE 7-1**
*Sources of Job Dissatisfaction*

Percent      Journalists are most dissatisfied with. . .

*(Bar chart with y-axis labeled in increments of 5 from 0 to 40, and four bars representing:)*
- Opportunities for training and professional development
- Pay and benefits
- Chances for promotion
- Ability to influence decisions affecting work life

and executives between Sept. 5 and Nov. 16, 2006.[2] This chapter will look at key findings of the survey and explore the future of newsroom training in America.

## HIGHLIGHTS: "INVESTING IN THE FUTURE OF NEWS"

1. *Journalists Need Training More than Ever.* Nine in 10 journalists feel they need more training than they are getting now. The top source of job discontent among them is "lack of training and development opportunities." Four in 10 say they are dissatisfied with training opportunities.

News executives agree that journalists need more training. Nine in 10 executives say their staffs would benefit from additional training. About half say their staffs would benefit "a lot."

2. *News Organizations Get Only a "C" Grade for Training.* Most journalists give their organizations no higher than an average grade for training. Executives give their training programs slightly higher marks. Both executives and staff give lower grades than they did five years ago.

**FIGURE 7-2**
*Training Report Cards*

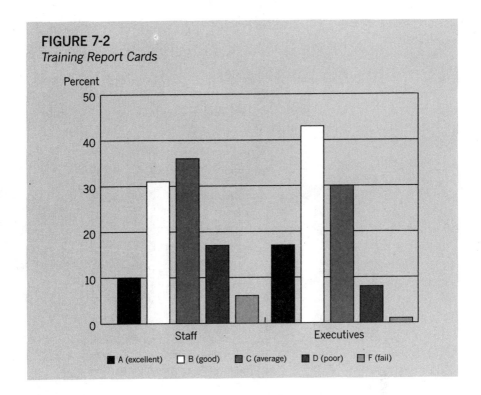

Percent

A (excellent)   B (good)   C (average)   D (poor)   F (fail)

3. *Training Is Uneven across the News Industry.* One in 10 news organizations provides no training, and three in 10 journalists are not provided with any training by their news organizations.

Executives say lack of money and time are the biggest obstacles to providing more training. On average, industry investment in training—time and money—is largely flat compared to 2002, except for a drop at the high end, among organizations spending $1,000 or more and allowing a staff member to be away for a month or more.

Four in 10 executives report that their newsroom training is part of a larger effort developed by a parent company, a higher rate than in 2002.

4. *News Organizations That Are Providing More Training Are Seeing Results.* Three in 10 news organizations have increased their training budgets in the past five years. Those increasing training tend to be national media organizations, the top 100 newspapers in circulation and smaller-market television outlets. Organizations in growth areas in the South and West were more likely to have increased training than news outlets in the Northeast or Midwest.

## FIGURE 7-3
*Investment in Training*

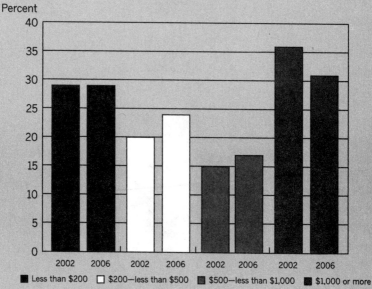

Most money the organization can spend per staff member per year

■ Less than $200   □ $200—less than $500   ▨ $500—less than $1,000   ▧ $1,000 or more

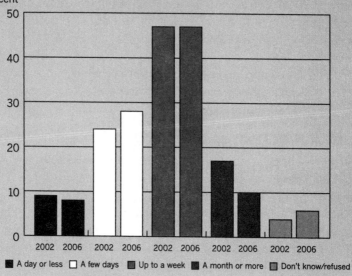

Most time away from work for a typical staff member to attend training per year

■ A day or less   □ A few days   ▨ Up to a week   ■ A month or more   ▧ Don't know/refused

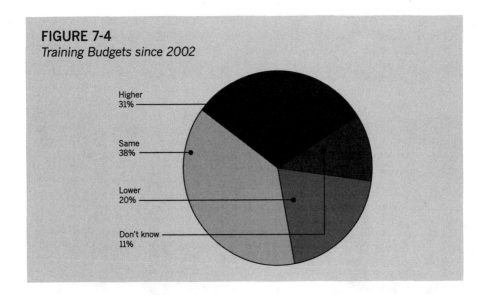

**FIGURE 7-4**
*Training Budgets since 2002*

Higher 31%

Same 38%

Lower 20%

Don't know 11%

Organizations that are increasing training tend to be more strategic about it: they are more likely to have a training coordinator, more likely to allocate 2 percent or more of their news budget to training, more likely to require staff members to participate in training and more likely to strongly link training to specific goals. Executives in these organizations give training performance an "A" or "B" grade.

Meanwhile, one in five news organizations has cut the training budget in the past five years and four in 10 are keeping training at about the same level.

5. *Weekly Newspapers, Local Radio and Ethnic Media Are Less Likely to Provide Training.* Local radio, weekly newspapers and ethnic media organizations tend to spend less money on training than larger organizations, suggesting they rely more on free training.

6. *Multimedia and New Media Training Are Increasing.* Training in ethics and law and in journalism crafts such as writing, photography and design are most often provided, executives say, followed by multimedia. Most news organizations plan to increase their spending for new media training. Content or beat training such as politics, business or health is provided less frequently, and the amount has declined since 2002.

Four in 10 journalists who feel they need additional training said they would benefit most from more training in new media, followed by craft skills (22 percent), beat areas (13 percent) and ethics (8 percent).

7. *Management Training Is a Priority.* Nine in 10 news executives want more training, and four in 10 say they would benefit most from management training. Their

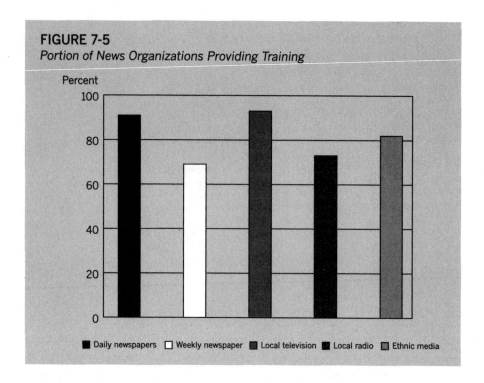

**FIGURE 7-5**
*Portion of News Organizations Providing Training*

Percent

Legend: ■ Daily newspapers ☐ Weekly newspaper ■ Local television ■ Local radio ▦ Ethnic media

staffs agree. Nine in 10 journalists also said top managers would benefit from additional training. Among staff who think top managers should have more training, more than half said they would benefit most from management training. Eight in 10 journalists said their immediate supervisors would benefit from more training, and nearly half said their supervisors needed management training more than any other type of training.

8. *Newsrooms Rely Most on In-House Training.* Eight in 10 news organizations provide in-house training. Six in 10 use outside programs. Journalists prefer outside pro-

**TABLE 7-1**
*Types of Training for Journalists*

|  | Craft skills | Ethics | New media | Content/beat |
|---|---|---|---|---|
| Organization provides training | 73% | 70% | 55% | 33% |
| Executives find training effective | 96 | 97 | 95 | 95 |
| Staff finds training useful | 87 | 90 | 92 | 93 |
| Organization plans to increase training | 29 | 22 | 54 | 26 |

**TABLE 7-2**
*Newsroom Usage of Training Programs*

|  | Used in last year |
| --- | --- |
| In-house or outside consultants in newsroom | 75% |
| Regional workshop by journalism organization | 66 |
| Regional conference of journalism organization | 63 |
| National conference of journalism organization | 60 |
| National workshop by journalism organization | 57 |
| Guides or other written materials from journalism organization or school | 57 |
| Web sites or listservs of journalism organization | 53 |
| Nonprofit journalism training center | 50 |
| Seminar by journalism school | 27 |
| Online distance learning | 25 |
| Yearlong university fellowship | 13 |

grams. Executives consider outside programs more effective in only one area—journalism ethics and legal issues.

9. *Use of Online Distance Learning Has Doubled.* One in 10 journalists uses online distance learning, compared to only 1 in 20 five years ago. The increase, which coincides with the development of Poynter's News University and its more than 32,000 registered users, is accompanied by greater interest in online learning on the part of news executives. More than two in 10 said their newsrooms had used this method in the past year and another four in 10 said they would seriously consider using it.

10. *Beginning Journalists Need More Training.* Only 3 percent of news executives who had recently hired new journalists said the new hires had the training they needed. More than half said new hires need some additional training, and four in 10 said new hires need a lot more training. Half of the executives cited journalism skills as the top training requirement.

## NEWSROOM LEARNING: A NEW DIVIDE?

Tomorrow's Workforce started in 2003 with $2 million from the Knight Foundation and a single question: Other professions invest heavily in training for their employees; why not the news industry?

The project also started with a simple hypothesis, the favorite scapegoat of cynical journalists: the problem was the profit-driven corporations that owned the newspapers.

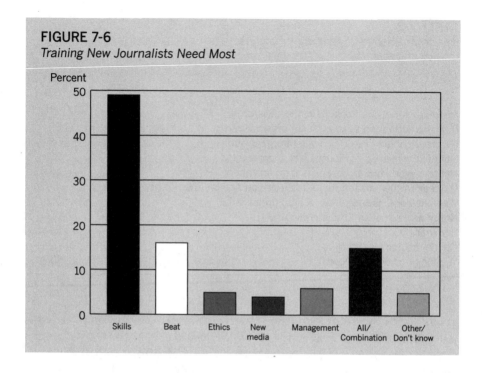

**FIGURE 7-6**
*Training New Journalists Need Most*

But we soon discovered the answer was more complex. Our work, along with that of other training projects in Knight's $10 million Newsroom Training Initiative, told a much more complicated story, one that is more promising because it looks to the future and not the past.

Yes, more money will help. But money alone won't satisfy journalists' deep hunger for the professional growth they need, and it won't fully prepare news organizations for an increasingly challenging media marketplace. A new question arose: "Can the news industry survive and thrive in the fast-changing new media marketplace when it relies primarily on scarce, random, charity-financed training?"

Our answer: not likely. So we began searching for a framework that would make training more effective and more deserving of resources because it could demonstrate a positive effect on news content and newsroom culture, both of which are linked to journalistic quality and greater audience appeal.

We asked newsroom executives and their staffs to help us answer questions such as: What are the goals of your training (and do top editors even agree on what they are)? How do you know you are meeting those goals? Is it more effective to send people away for training or bring trainers to the newsroom? How much training do you actually offer? Can you find ways to train without waiting for money that never comes? Do employees understand what they are supposed to do with what they have learned? What roles do newsroom executives and frontline editors play in making training effective? What training do top editors themselves need to accomplish this goal? What role does newsroom culture play in fostering learning and change? What role does training play in improving newsroom culture? How will training help transform the newsroom from a static, defensive organization to a nimble, constructive one?

Answers to these questions determined a new goal for Tomorrow's Workforce: to identify and explore with partner newsrooms the elements and practices that can—and have—made training for journalism professionals more effective both for the individual journalists and the organizations they serve. We ended with a framework that we believe can help newsrooms conceive more effective training and prove they are working in ways that serve great journalism and strategies to gather larger audiences for news.

We laid out that framework in the chapters of this book: Lead and communicate. Set goals and measure progress. Improve culture. Involve staff. Make the news more readable, useful, convenient, relevant. Train. Teach. Learn. Innovate. And then train some more. Repeat continuously.

That last point cannot be emphasized enough. Consider what happened to media just during the span of our project. Thousands of journalists lost their jobs, including several high-profile editors. Many more thousands of newspaper readers switched from print to digital. Google became the world's biggest media company. YouTube was born (and sold 18 months later for $1.6 billion, to Google). Knight Ridder died, the legendary company's 32 newspapers scattered.

These events, and a steady parade of others, changed the conversation about change. As good a tipping point as any is Rupert Murdoch's powerful I-got-religion-and-you-better-get-it-too speech to the American Society of Newspaper Editors at its 2005 convention. Murdoch scolded the editors for "quietly hoping"— as he once did—"that this thing called the digital revolution would just limp along." He continued:

> The peculiar challenge, then, is for us digital immigrants . . . to apply a digital mindset to a new set of challenges. We need to realize that the next generation of people accessing news and information, whether from newspapers or any other source, has a different set of expectations about the kind of news they will get, including when and how they will get it, where they will get it from, and who they will get it from. . . . Unless we awaken to these changes . . . we will, as an industry, be relegated to the status of also-rans.

Today, and in coming years, journalists and their institutions face fundamental questions about their responsibility to society in an era of economic upheaval. To these huge questions we add one simple point: The future of news will belong to those who build it. And if you don't know how, it's time to learn.

Our framework for strategic change offers a set of tools that news companies and newsrooms can use to become learning organizations, with the capacity to grow and improve, constantly looking for the next of the thousands of steps that lead to a future.

Tomorrow's Workforce advised 17 newsrooms in 2004–2006, large (*The Atlanta Journal-Constitution*, *The Oregonian* and the South Florida *Sun-Sentinel*) and small (the *Waco Tribune-Herald*, the *La Crosse [Wis.] Tribune* and *The Dothan [Ala.] Eagle*).

We sought partners who said they wanted change. Then we urged them to learn to change even more.

"I think the project pushed me to more directly address the need for overall change in the newsroom," said Sandy Rowe, editor of *The Oregonian*. "Despite the difficulty of changing the status quo and the risks inherent in doing so, this project has helped the newsroom leadership team see the necessity for change and potential for great improvement."

The good news is that more daily newspaper editors like Rowe are taking over change by investing in strategic training, editorial innovation and collaborative efforts to improve newsroom culture; the bad news is that too many others still are not. Despite increased investment in training at many of the newspapers involved in Tomorrow's Workforce and the other projects funded by the Knight Newsroom Training Initiative, too many newspapers persist in undertraining their workforce.

Knight's training survey found that the average newsroom spends no more on training today than it did five years ago despite growing evidence that training fuels innovation. And the Inland Press Association, as we mentioned in chapter 6, reports that the amount of money newspapers spend on training actually fell during the same period from 0.6 to 0.4 percent of payroll. (Remember, the national spending average for all industries is 2.3 percent.)[3]

Corporate leaders including McClatchy's Gary Pruitt and Cox's Jay Smith have spoken about the critical need to train midcareer journalists. The corporations they lead, as well as others, including Gannett, Lee Enterprises and Scripps, have stepped up and provided training to their member newsrooms. Corporations also funded the Southern Newspaper Publishers' Association Traveling Campus and have lent support to training centers such as the American Press Institute.

But these good efforts fall far short of a systematic, strategic, newsroom-based approach traditional news organizations need if they are to vault into the new media era. These efforts sit atop an industrywide attitude that training is for the most part a nice thing that charities give away, not a primary responsibility—and indeed the business necessity—of owners.

Karen Brown Dunlap, president of The Poynter Institute, says that mindset is lamentable:

There's a long-term picture of the industry not spending much on training. Then more recently you have a significant amount of money for training come from philanthropic organizations. That's a shame. It's a shame these (news) organizations don't want to invest in the people who serve them.

. . . I'm hearing so much about cutting, cutting, cutting. When you remind them that there's value in training, some will pause to try to make sure there are funds for training. The large number are so concerned now about the bottom line that they will continue to cut training.

Relying solely on free or heavily discounted training from nonprofit organizations like Poynter and the American Press Institute isn't acceptable. "You can learn a lot from Poynter Online," says Dunlap. "You can take a NewsU course and most of them are no cost. Very often the industry is content to assume that that takes care of the whole need—which it does not. The industry needs a continuum of training, from individual efforts to long-term off-site training."

If the owners don't come through, local publishers and top newsroom editors have the means to provide more training in their newsrooms. In chapter 4, we told of newsrooms that increased their training significantly without large dollar budgets.

Instead, these editors made a choice. As Julia D. Wallace of *The Atlanta Journal-Constitution* said, "The time and focus is the real resource, not the money."

Those who live in the mindset of time deprivation that pervades newsrooms may find this hard to imagine or accept. But organizations, even newsrooms, have a way of getting the most important things done. Small newsrooms in Waco, Dothan and La Crosse found ways to provide their staffs with a lot of training because their top editors decided it would happen. Somehow, even with hundreds of hours of training, their newspapers still came out every day and got better, and their Web sites got updated even more frequently and got better too. If training is important, all it really takes is leadership and will.

"The concept that 'we don't do much training in our newsroom because we don't have the money for it' is absolutely a crutch and is a big cop-out in a large way," says John Smalley, editor of the 32,000-circulation *Tribune* in La Crosse, Wisc. "We found if you pay attention to the idea of 'what do we need help with and how can we get that help' there are many ways of getting that help without spending tons of money."

Smalley's comment was in stark contrast with what we often heard from top editors. And the idea that the will to train might be more important than the dollar budget was a key lesson for us, and we hope it will be an empowering one for many top editors.

Another lesson was the power of group learning in the newsroom to transform content and culture. We hope that lesson will encourage training organizations, as well as newsrooms, to develop more ways of training groups of journalists with their colleagues in their newsrooms.

Some of that work is under way. Poynter's Jill Geisler, for example, worked intensively with senior editors and team leaders at *The Oregonian*, a Tomorrow's Workforce partner. That group showed progress in moving toward more constructive behavior, a change unlikely to have been accomplished if the newspaper was only able to send a few editors each year away for training.

Training in the newsroom is often seen as a poor alternative to training off-site. Our partner newsrooms demonstrated that is not always the case.

In newsroom surveys, we saw that staff opinion of in-house training became more positive once it was linked to goals, developed with staff input and made interactive. The traditional gap that has journalists rating outside training as more effective than in-house training began to close.

Poynter added significantly to journalists' training options with creation of the Knight-funded News University. NewsU drew more than 32,000 registered users in less than two years, underscoring the demand for quality training among journalists.

We believe each newspaper should set its own training priorities based on the uniqueness of its staff, its market and its goals. Yet industry leaders also see a need to concentrate professional development in areas that will help newspapers in the process of reinvention.

Mary Nesbitt of the Readership Institute places the learning needs of newsrooms into four buckets:

- *Craft and skills.* "Which is huge, and gets bigger every day. Now it's cross-platform."

- *Managerial and human relations.* "How to function in an organization and work with others."

- *Business literacy.* "All the external things that affect the business: market conditions, economics, audience."

- *Creativity, innovation and product development.* "Learn how to create the things that are going to drive our business forward and assure that we have a future."

Only three in 100 editors who have hired new journalists felt the new hires were fully prepared and did not need more training. Granted, many of those entering the newsroom have not been to journalism school, and we don't embrace the idea that journalists can come from school a finished product that never needs more training.

Still, journalism academics must play an important role in advancing training for journalism students and professional journalists. And, like news organizations, journalism schools must act quickly, far more quickly than the pace of change to which most academic institutions are accustomed.

And what does all this mean for journalists? For now, many are on their own in preparing for the future. There is not enough education, training and professional development to meet the needs we found in our poll and heard in our more than 500 newsroom interviews. Things are improving in some newsrooms, yes, but individual journalists yearning for growth must sign on with the media organizations that are making concrete efforts to adapt and invest in their staff. Look out for your own learning. Learn to change.

And learning to change is work. All editors we interviewed for this book spoke about the difficulty of undergoing personal change, of revamping their leadership style and of the challenges in moving their newsrooms toward innovation. But they also spoke of the rewards of change, the engagement of their staffs and the new content in the newspaper and online.

It's work, but it's work that must be done, say industry leaders, including Pruitt of McClatchy:

> Creating cultures that are comfortable with change and uncertainty—those are imperatives. That learning has to be part of almost every activity we pursue. That's really something that's scary, but it can be challenging and fun. What I always try to tell the people at McClatchy is that we're going to be OK. We're going to be fine. We're going to get through any difficulty within the industry. I don't know exactly how it's going to go, but we're going to have the right values, we're going to do the best we can, we're going to try to be fair and equitable, and we're all going to participate. We're just going to have to adjust and learn as we go along. We're going to be in it together.

Learn. Adjust. Learn some more. Adapt. Change. Imagine a different kind of future for journalism. Imagine industry executives who talk as proudly of investing in their people, their process and their products as they do of their operating profits. Imagine newsrooms whose leaders and staffs see the possibilities of innovation and who have the skills needed to accomplish them. Imagine news organizations so connected to their communities that citizens see them as powerful—and necessary—tools for maintaining civil society. Imagine it, and work toward it.

As Eric Newton says in the introduction to this book, "Media evolution doesn't favor the big or strong. It favors the nimble. Be nimble."

Good advice for anyone in journalism—corporate executives, top editors, journalists of all types, journalism educators and students. Learn to be nimble.

## CHAPTER 1

*Epigraph:* David Zeeck, speech to American Society of Newspaper Editors convention, April 20, 2006, Seattle, Wash.

1. Impact Study (Evanston, Ill.: Readership Institute, 2001).
2. Meyer was a consultant to Tomorrow's Workforce and the Learning Newsroom.
3. "Reaching New Readers: Revolution, Not Evolution" (Evanston, Ill.: Readership Institute, 2004).
4. Antonellis was a consultant to the Learning Newsroom.
5. Jeffrey Pfeffer and Robert I. Sutton, *The Knowing-Doing Gap* (Boston: Harvard Business School Press, 2000), 1.
6. Poynter Institute, www.poynter.org/subject.asp?id=14.
7. Michael Smith, "Take the Risk, Reap the Reward" (Evanston, Ill.: Readership Institute, April 26, 2006).
8. Greg Jarboe, Search Engine Watch, "Beyond Beta: Google News Graduates," Jan. 25, 2006.
9. Zeeck, speech to American Society of Newspaper Editors.
10. Ibid.
11. "Newsroom Training: Where's the Investment?" John S. and James L. Knight Foundation, 2002, 9.
12. U.S. Small Business Administration, www.sba.gov/smallbusinessplanner/manage/lead/index.html.
13. John P. Kotter, *A Force for Change* (New York: MacMillan, 1990), 4.
14. Daniel Goleman, Richard Boyatzis and Annie McKee, *Primal Leadership, Realizing the Power of Emotional Intelligence* (Boston: Harvard Business School Press, 2002), 5.
15. Steve Buttry, American Press Institute, "Sometimes It's Not Nice to Be Nice, and Other Lessons for Editors," www.americanpressinstitute.org/pages/resources/2006/04/sometimes_its_not_nice_to_be_n/ (April 23, 2006).
16. John P. Kotter, *Leading Change* (Boston: Harvard Business School Press, 1996), 68–69.
17. James C. Collins and Jerry I. Porras, *Built to Last: Successful Habits of Visionary Companies* (New York: HarperCollins, 1994), 201.
18. Ibid., 199–200.
19. Charles Horton Cooley, *Human Nature and the Social Order* (New York: Charles Scribner's Sons, 1922), 328.
20. Kotter, *A Force for Change.*

21. Daniel Goleman et al, *Primal Leadership* (Boston: Harvard Business School Press, 2002).

**CHAPTER 2**

*Epigraph:* James C. Collins and Jerry I. Porras, *Built to Last: Successful Habits of Visionary Companies* (New York: HarperCollins, 1994), 11.

1. Peter M. Senge, *The Fifth Discipline* (New York: Doubleday, 1990), 213.
2. Collins and Porras, *Built to Last*, 185.
3. Steven Duke, "Small Newspapers Make Big Changes," Readership Institute, June 8, 2006, www.readership.org/blog2/2006/06/small-newspapers-make-big-changes.html.
4. Ibid.
5. John Robinson, "Happy New Year: Our News-Agenda for 2006," *News & Record*, Jan. 1, 2006.
6. John P. Kotter and Dan Cohen, *The Heart of Change* (Boston: Harvard Business School Press, 2002), 2.

**CHAPTER 3**

1. "Inside Newspaper Culture," Readership Institute, Northwestern University, 2000, www.readership.org.
2. John P. Kotter and James L. Heskett, "Corporate Culture and Performance" (New York: The Free Press, 1992), 141.
3. Impact Study, Readership Institute, 2000, www.readership.org.
4. Ibid.
5. "Inside Newspaper Culture," Readership Institute.
6. Kotter and Heskett, "Corporate Culture and Performance," 142.
7. William Damon and Brett Mueller, "Committee of Concerned Journalists Traveling Curriculum Assessment Report," June 2006, 83.
8. Human Synergistics International, www.humansynergistics.com/site, copyright 2006, adapted by permission.
9. Damon and Mueller, "Committee of Concerned Journalists Traveling Curriculum Assessment Report," 56.
10. William Damon and Brett Mueller, "Improving Newsroom Communication," *The American Editor*, January 2006, 23–24.
11. Interview by Vickey Williams, the Learning Newsroom.
12. *The Hamilton Spectator* Learning Newsroom Steering Committee.
13. Libby Averyt, "Quick Reaction Was No Accident," *Presstime*, Newspaper Association of America, April 2006.
14. The survey instrument was the Organizational Culture Inventory®, developed by Human Synergistics, Inc., of Arlington Heights, Ill. The instrument has been used to assess culture in thousands of organizations around the world and has

been administered to approximately 3 million people. Seven newsrooms were part of Tomorrow's Workforce; six were part of the Learning Newsroom.

15. Ibid.

## CHAPTER 4

1. Peter M. Senge, *The Fifth Discipline: The Art and Practice of the Learning Organization* (New York: Doubleday, 1990), 234–235.
2. Jeanne C. Meister, *Corporate Universities: Lessons in Building a World-Class Work Force* (New York: McGraw-Hill, 1998), 21.
3. Ibid.
4. Ibid., 22.
5. Ibid., 12–13.
6. A great source of tips and information about trainers and training is the News Coach list-serv, www.poynter.org.

## CHAPTER 5

1. Jacqui Banaszynski, Report for the Frontline Editor Project, November 2005.
2. John Greenman, "Hearing about Editors' Difficulties Trying to Find Solutions," Neiman Reports.
3. Quy Nguyen Huy, "In Praise of Middle Managers," Harvard Business School Publishing Corporation, September 2001, 73.
4. Ibid.
5. Ibid.
6. Greenman, "Hearing about Editors' Difficulties."
7. Ibid.
8. John Greenman, Study of 2004–2005 NewsTrain participants, July 30, 2006.

## CHAPTER 6

1. Newspaper Next, "Blueprint for Transformation," Sept. 27, 2006, http://newspapernext.org.
2. Newspaper Association of America, "Who Killed the Newspaper?" *Economist*, Aug. 24, 2006.
3. Laurie Bassi, Karen McGraw and Daniel McMurrer, "Beyond Quarterly Earnings: Using Measurement to Create Sustainable Growth" (Atlanta, Ga.: McBassi & Company, September 2003); Bruce Pfau and Ira Kay of Watson Wyatt write: "Organizations with the best human capital practices provide returns to shareholders that are three times greater than those of companies with weak human capital practices," from *The Human Capital Edge* (New York: McGraw Hill, 2002).
4. Laurie Bassi and Daniel McMurrer, "What to Do When People Are Your Most Important Asset" (Atlanta, Ga.: McBassi & Company, May 2004).

5. American Society for Training and Development, 2005 State of the Industry Report, December 2005.

6. Paul Farhi, "Under Siege," *American Journalism Review* (February/March 2006).

7. Readership Institute, "The Business Case for People Management" (Evanston, Ill.: Readership Institute, July 2000), 6.

8. Ibid.

9. "Preparing the Workforce," in *TD Magazine*, September 2006.

10. Great Place to Work Institute, "From Great to Best: Culture as a Competitive Advantage in Healthcare," June 21, 2006.

11. Ibid.

12. Accenture News, "Talent Wars Shift from Crusade for Acquisition to Battle for Retention," March 21, 2001 (http://newsroom.accenture.com/article_display.cfm?article_id=3702

13. Accenture, "The High-Performance Workforce Study," 2002–2003.

14. Newspaper Association of America, "Preserving Talent II" (2003).

15. Ibid.

16. Readership Institute, "The Business Case for People Management."

17. Ibid.

18. Newspaper Association of America, "Preserving Talent II."

19. Accenture News, "Talent Wars Shift from Crusade for Acquisition to Battle for Retention."

20. Readership Institute, www.readership.org/culture_management/culture/inside culture.asp.

21. The 2005 U.S. industry average is 2.3 percent, according to the American Society for Training & Development; the 2005 newspaper industry average is 0.4 percent, according to the Inland Press Association.

22. Wikipedia, http://en.wikipedia.org/wiki/Bakotopia.

23. Mary Nesbitt, "Editors: Would You Do This to Your A-Section?" (Evanston, Ill.: Readership Institute, Oct. 23, 2006).

24. Readership Institute, "Reaching New Readers: Revolution, Not Evolution" (Evanston, Ill.: Readership Institute, July 2004).

**CHAPTER 7**

1. John S. and James L. Knight Foundation, "Newsroom Training: Where's the Investment?" (Miami, Fl.: Knight Foundation, April 2002), 9.

2. Margin of error, editors/news executives' survey is plus or minus 5 percentage points; staff survey is plus or minus 3 percentage points. Survey methodology is available at www.newsimproved.org.

3. American Society for Training and Development, 2005 State of the Industry Report, December 2005.

# Recommended Reading

Bridges, William (Managing Transitions). *Making the Most of Change*. Da Capo Press, 2003.

Christensen, Clayton M. *The Innovator's Dilemma*. FirstHarper Business Essentials, 2003.

Collins, James C. and Porras, Jerry I. *Built to Last: Successful Habits of Visionary Companies*. HarperCollins, 1994.

Collins, Jim. *Good to Great: Why Some Companies Make the Leap . . . and Others Don't*. HarperCollins, 2001.

Gordon, Rich. *Can Newspapers Be Saved?* 2006, www.readership.org.

Heifetz, Ronald A. and Linsky, Martin. *Leadership on the Line: Staying Alive through the Dangers of Leading*. Harvard Business School Press, 2002.

Kline, Peter and Saunders, Bernard. *Ten Steps to a Learning Organization*. Great Ocean Publisher, 1993.

Kotter, John P. *A Force for Change: How Leadership Differs from Management*. The Free Press, 1990.

Kotter, John P. *Leading Change*. Harvard Business School Press, 1996.

Kotter, John P. and Heskett, James L. *Corporate Culture and Performance*. The Free Press, 1992.

Kotter, John P. and Rathgeber, Holger. *Our Iceberg Is Melting: Changing and Succeeding Under Any Conditions*. St. Martin's Press, 2005.

Lencioni, Patrick M. *The Five Dysfunctions of a Team: A Leadership Fable*. Jossey-Bass, 2002.

Meister, Jeanne C. (American Society for Training and Development). *Corporate Universities: Lessons in Building a World-Class Workforce*. McGraw-Hill, 1998.

Meyer, Phillip. *The Vanishing Newspaper: Saving Journalism in the Information Age*. University of Missouri Press, 2004.

Newspaper Association of America. "Preserving Talent: Part II," 2003. www.naa.org/diversity/preservingtalent2.pdf.

Newton, Eric, ed. *Newsroom Training: Where's the Investment? A Study of the Council of Presidents of National Journalism Organizations*. Knight Foundation, Miami, Fl., 2002.

Pfeffer, Jeffrey and Sutton, Robert I. *The Knowing-Doing Gap, How Smart Companies Turn Knowledge into Action*. Harvard Business School Press, 1999.

Readership Institute. "The Business Case for People Management," 2000. www.readership.org/culture_management/people_mgt/data/business_case.pdf.

Readership Institute. Essential Background/About Experiences. www.readership.org.

Readership Institute. "Inside Newspaper Culture," 2000. www.readership.org/culture_management/culture/insideculture.asp.

Senge, Peter; Kleiner, Art; Roberts, Charlotte; Ross, Richard; Roth, George and Smith, Bryan. *The Dance of Change: The Challenges of Sustaining Momentum in Learning Organizations*. Doubleday, 1999.

Silberman, Mel. *Active Learning: 101 Strategies to Teach Any Subject*. Allyn and Bacon, 1996.

Silberman, Mel. *Active Training: A Handbook of Techniques, Designs, Case Examples, and Tips*. Jossey-Bass/Pfeiffer, 1998.

Silberman, Mel. *101 Ways to Make Training Active*. John Wiley & Sons, Inc., 2005.

Stolovitch, Harold. *Telling Ain't Training*. American Society for Training and Development, 2002.

# The Learning Matrix

**A**t Tomorrow's Workforce we learned the value of going beyond the surface on training needs, considering more options than the staff or executives might most readily suggest.

Our hypothesis was that training would be more effective if considered in the context of goals, leadership and staff capacity, newsroom practices and communications and other factors.

To assess these things, we typically visited newsrooms at least twice, conducting:

- Interviews with top editors focusing on journalistic and readership goals of the newsroom, successes and challenges.

- Interviews with staff and middle managers that focused on perceptions of the leadership, whether goals were clearly understood, and examples of practices that led staff members to hear mixed messages. In small newsrooms, we often interviewed the entire staff; in large metros, we interviewed at least 20 percent of the staff.

- Reviews of available market and readership research and demographics in light of leadership goals.

- Content analysis keyed to goals.

Working with evaluations consultant Michael Quinn Patton of Minneapolis, we developed a Learning Matrix, a report of about 25 pages designed to help newsroom executives think about goals in broad context and to prioritize immediate training goals and long-term ones. Here are short, edited excerpts from different reports that illustrate the system and reflect issues that we found to be fairly typical in newsrooms.

## INTRODUCTION

This report is based on interviews with staff members, market and demographic data, the cultural assessment of the newsroom and an analysis of the newspaper's content.

The report is organized by elements of the newspaper and of the newsroom:

- Strengths and Assets—The foundation on which to build.
- Content—What the reader sees.

- Business Operations and Newsroom Impact—The economic circumstances in which the newsroom operates.
- Mission and Priorities—The goals and the objectives of the newspaper.
- Organizational Culture—The "personality" of the newsroom, as determined by the Organizational Culture Inventory® survey.
- Staff Capacity and Characteristics—The skills, attitudes and desires of the rank and file.
- Management Capacity and Characteristics—The skills, attitudes and desires of midlevel managers.
- Leadership Capacity and Characteristics—The skills, attitudes and desires of the top newsroom executives.
- Learning and Professional Development—Training capacity and needs.

Each section of the report has five components, the first four of which are contained in a grid called the Learning Matrix:

- Findings—Observations and collected data.
- Implications—What the findings could mean to the newsroom.
- Learning Options—Suggestions for training to address the findings.
- Results—Goals that might be achieved through the training.
- Notes—Clips from the interviews or research that illustrate the findings.

## Strengths and Assets

| Findings | Implications | Learning Options | Results |
|---|---|---|---|
| Staff members enjoy their jobs and are willing to contribute more to the success of the newspaper. | Positive acceptance of change. Ready pool of volunteers. Potential frustration if goodwill is misused or ignored. | Involve staff in discussion, decision and planning stages of all newsroom initiatives. | Knowledge transfer from veterans to less experienced staff. More engagement, and thus buy-in, on newsroom initiatives. |
| Newsroom employees express a high degree of peer-to-peer respect. | Staff is willing to learn from each other. There are natural newsroom leaders who can be involved in quality initiatives. | Create peer-to-peer learning programs. Establish mentoring system for younger staff members. Draw on staff expertise to shape training curriculum. | More interaction, thus collaboration, among staff. Cost-effective, in-house learning. Better development of younger staff members. |

## Content

| Findings | Implications | Learning Options | Results |
|---|---|---|---|
| There is a strong emphasis on local news—more than half of the stories in the newspaper are local. | Community news is a priority. | Ongoing evaluation, through surveys and informal discussion, of what type of local news connects most with readers. Ongoing discussion of Readership Institute findings as applied to local content. | More awareness of impact of the paper on readers. |
| A high percentage of local news stories are process or institution oriented; ordinary people stories are rare. | Newspaper seems stuffy, institutional. News pages don't reflect the diversity of the community. Readers who are not interested in government news may look elsewhere for news of their interests. | Develop story-planning strategies that seek out people stories. Re-examine beat priorities. Explore new story forms that minimize process but still report the news. | A more "people-friendly" product. Less emphasis on institutions, more on people. |
| Traditional journalistic writing styles dominate stories and headlines. | Headlines and ledes may not draw in readers. More creative writers are frustrated by adherence to rigid forms. News content lacks personality. | Celebrate the best writing. Create and discuss common standards for good headline and story writing. Train line editors to coach reporters. Explore new story forms for institutional stories. | More varied writing in the paper. Better headlines. Less frustration among best writers. |
| Diversity of the community is not reflected in the content. | At best, lack of attraction to minority readers. At worst, alienation of those readers. | Tours of minority neighborhoods. Meetings with community leaders. New source development by reporters. Redefinition of beat coverage | Better reflection of the community. |

## Content Notes

- We're a "little too stiff and formal and gray—and tedious. . . . We do a lot of stories because we can—or we think we should." The paper has an obligatory nature. "Stories are edited to be safe . . . the wit and style is edited out."—Reporter, veteran.

- Process and government stories—several mentions. "We're from the open receptacle school of journalism. We seem to be on top of government issues to a fault. We do a lot of process."—Midlevel editor.

## Business Operations and Newsroom Impact

| Findings | Implications | Learning Options | Results |
|---|---|---|---|
| Circulation is increasing, driven by the strong growth in both the region and the newspaper's primary market areas. However, ad revenue is not keeping pace and could decline in the next fiscal year. | As ad revenue falls, newsroom budget likely to decrease. Suburban growth may force newsroom to choose which set of readers to go after. | Examine beat structure and definition annually to determine resource allocation and coverage priorities. Share and discuss market and readership information with newsroom. | Better understanding of changing community. Culture of change and flexibility in deploying resources. Common understanding of the community and readership patterns. |

## Organizational Culture

| Findings | Implications | Learning Options | Results |
|---|---|---|---|
| The culture of the newsroom is mostly defensive. Main behaviors are perfectionism (avoid mistakes at all costs) and opposition (confrontation prevails, even passively.) | Newsroom is risk averse. Constructive cultures are more adaptive, have higher readership, defensive ones less likely to engage audiences. | Create more collaborative opportunities. Include all segments of the newsroom in planning new editorial initiatives. | A more adaptive, nimble workforce. |
| Newsroom is considered a collegial place to | Lack of discussion or feedback about weak- | Create opportunities to discuss, evaluate and | More feedback for staff. (continues) |

## Organizational Culture (continued)

| Findings | Implications | Learning Options | Results |
|---|---|---|---|
| work, perhaps too nice. | nesses or differences inhibits improvement and change. | challenge assumptions about content of the paper. Reward risk-taking. Create opportunities for critical self-assessment of the news product. Set annual goals for individual staff members. | Better sense of collective values. More open environment for criticism. |

## Staff Capacity and Characteristics

| Findings | Implications | Learning Options | Results |
|---|---|---|---|
| Staff is highly accomplished and possesses a wide range of journalistic skills. | High capacity for excellent work. | Use the staff's expertise to teach subjects desired by other staff members— CAR, beat and source development. | Better-skilled staff members at all levels. |
| Staff wants more feedback on performance. | Editors are not providing sufficient feedback. Reporters are unsure of their status or the quality of their work. | Train editors to coach better. Set and follow up on annual goals | More communication between reporters and editors. More coaching, direction and feedback. |

## Management Capacity and Characteristics

| Findings | Implications | Learning Options | Results |
|---|---|---|---|
| Midlevel editors are respected, but seen by some as having little authority. | Lines of authority are less clear, so decisionmaking is impeded and confidence in line editors is eroded. Some editors and reporters will | Clarify roles of midlevel editors vs. those of leadership team. Create an opportunity among managers and leadership to discuss and evaluate | Clearer roles. Structure that takes advantage of strengths and minimizes weaknesses of key managers. |

(continues)

## Management Capacity and Characteristics (continued)

| Findings | Implications | Learning Options | Results |
|---|---|---|---|
| | wait to see which way management is leaning before acting. | newsroom structure. Adjust accordingly. Offer training in managing up to midlevel editors. | |
| There is a sense of mixed messages from leadership at the staff and middle manager level. | Confusion about direction of newspaper can lead to inaction or further aversion to change until managers and staff know which is the "right" way to go. | Clarify priorities for the paper. Connect priorities to individual and team goals. Create ongoing opportunities to discuss and evaluate the effect of those priorities on the news product. | Better understanding of the direction and of the standards of the paper. |

## Management Notes

COMMUNICATION

- "They are smart people who have the newspaper's best interest at heart and place the interests of the staff after that. . . . They don't realize the impact their decisions have on people who are slogging it out."—Editor.

- "The middle managers don't have enough authority. . . . They are pressed from the top."—Reporter.

## Leadership Capacity and Characteristics

| Findings | Implications | Learning Options | Results |
|---|---|---|---|
| Leadership has little transparency for staff into the thinking behind goals or changes in direction. | Confusion among staff and middle managers about direction of the paper leads to inaction or cautious behavior. | Leadership team discussion to focus priorities. Create opportunities for staff members to be involved in implementation of priorities. | Less confusion about priorities. Clearer understanding of how to implement them. Greater buy-in of— or at least transparency into— leadership initiatives. |

(continues)

*Leadership Capacity and Characteristics (continued)*

| Findings | Implications | Learning Options | Results |
|---|---|---|---|
| | | Create ongoing means of communication between leadership and staff, emphasizing personal communications. | |
| Communication of priorities and goals is not as effective as leadership team would like. | Newsroom leaders may assume staff members are actively resisting change when they may not understand the goal or how to apply it in their role. More coaching may be needed. | Communications and teaching-skills training for leadership team. | Better understanding by staff and managers of leadership goals. |

*Leadership Notes*

- "We don't feel a consistent message of priorities from management. We're at a point now where the paper really isn't clear what direction it wants to go."—Editor.

- We have no "understanding of why big decisions are made. . . . The midlevel editors go into that meeting in the morning and say, 'OK, that's it. Here's your marching orders.'"—Reporter.

*Learning and Professional Development*

| Findings | Implications | Learning Options | Results |
|---|---|---|---|
| The newsroom has an ambitious training schedule but attendance is below desired level. | Training may not fit needs or desires of staff. | Seek input from staff on training needs and effectiveness of current training. Make some sessions mandatory. | More buy-in from staff on training initiatives. Higher attendance. Better understanding of what training is working. |

(continues)

*Learning and Professional Development (continued)*

| Findings | Implications | Learning Options | Results |
|---|---|---|---|
| Staff input on training schedule is minimal. | Training may be seen as management responsibility, not that of staff. | Create newsroom training committee of staff members co-ordinated by training/recruitment director. | More input from staff. Better understanding by management of staff priorities. Shift in responsibility for training from "them" to "us." |

We found this information helped partner newsrooms revisit their goals and priorities in context of process and people issues that might encourage or inhibit learning. (For a form you can use, visit our Web site, www.newsimproved.org.)

**Michele McLellan** is the founder and director of Tomorrow's Workforce, a $2.2 million research and development project funded by the John S. and James L. Knight Foundation in 2003–2007. McLellan previously was an editor and manager in newspapers for 25 years, most recently at *The Oregonian* in Portland, Ore., from 1984–2003. While at *The Oregonian*, McLellan served as politics editor, ombudsman and special projects editor with emphasis on building better interaction among citizens, newspaper readers and the newsroom.

She also has taught and spoken about journalism ethics and credibility, nationally and internationally, and is the primary author of *The Newspaper Credibility Handbook*, published by the American Society of Newspaper Editors in 2001. A former Nieman Fellow at Harvard University (2001–2002), she has taught journalism at Harvard and at Royal University in Phnom Penh, Cambodia.

McLellan divides her time between the United States and Cambodia.

**Tim Porter** is an editor and writer with an extensive background in print and digital journalism. He is associate director of Tomorrow's Workforce. Porter was founding editor of Examiner.com, the online operation of the *San Francisco Examiner*. He was also assistant managing editor for news, metro editor and business editor for the *Examiner*. Earlier, Porter was editor of the *Richmond Independent*, a 45,000-circulation daily in the San Francisco Bay area.

Porter has also worked with information-intensive companies such as Goldman Sachs, Charles Schwab and Glass, Lewis, providing consulting on financial services, research, product development and workflow. He is the author of First Draft, a blog devoted to journalism quality, innovation and strategic change.

Porter lives in Mill Valley, Calif.

## The Knight Foundation

The John S. and James L. Knight Foundation, founded with the personal fortunes of newspaper owners Jack and Jim Knight, has given more than $300 million to journalism-related causes since 1950. It aims to advance journalism excellence through education and training, to promote press freedom at home and abroad and to help improve news in the public interest in all its forms.

The Knight Foundation seeks opportunities to invest in high-impact, transformational projects that create visible, lasting change. If all goes as planned, its newest project, the Knight Brothers' 21st Century News Challenge, will set aside $25 million over the next five years to seed innovative community news experiments. In the 20th century, the Knight Brothers' newspapers were the glue that helped bind and build communities; Knight wants to know who or what will be its successor in the 21st. (You can learn more about the contest at www.newschallenge.org.) Why focus on local news? Because our democracy is organized by community; our future as a nation cannot be separated from that of our towns, suburbs and cities.

In 2002–2003, the Knight Foundation approved a total of $10 million in grants for its Newsroom Training Initiative to increase awareness of the importance of training among journalists and to explore ways to make it more effective. Eric Newton, designer of the foundation's Newsroom Training Initiative, served as an editor of *News, Improved*.

Knight has supported dozens of important journalism groups that offer training, but the six projects described below were different: each had a significant research and development component to study and increase the effectiveness of training. We have drawn heavily on the work of these projects and their leaders in writing *News, Improved*.

## News University at The Poynter Institute

Launched in April 2005 with a $2.8 million grant from Knight, News University (NewsU) pioneered online training for the news industry. NewsU's highly interactive modules attracted more than 32,000 journalists, students and educators in 157 countries in less than two years.

By 2007 NewsU (www.newsu.org) was offering more than 30 e-learning courses that appeal to journalists at all levels of experience and in all types of media. Most are free or low-cost. They include such titles as Cleaning Your Copy, Get Me Rewrite: The Craft of Revision, Color in News Design, Handling Race and Ethnicity, Math for Journalists, Freedom of Information, On-Line Project Development and Beat Basics and Beyond. A complete course list is available at www.newsu.org/courselist.

User evaluations since 2005 show NewsU effectively meeting the training needs of journalists.

- 73 percent said their course was useful to extremely useful.

- 87 percent said they were likely to participate in another course.

- 75 percent said they would recommend NewsU to a colleague.

- 63 percent said they were likely to use the course as a reference in the future.

Howard Finberg, director of Interactive Learning and NewsU at Poynter, offered his follow-up research as well as significant wisdom and encouragement in developing *News, Improved*.

### The Traveling Curriculum of the Committee of Concerned Journalists (CCJ)

These newsroom workshops focus on helping journalists to become more reflective in their work and to develop their capacity for critical thinking. They raise newsroom standards and improve communication.

The program grew out of years of discussion with more than a thousand journalists concerned about the future of the profession and what they saw as a rise in "infotainment" and personal opinion in the news. In 2003 the project received a grant of $2 million from the Knight Foundation to take the workshops on the road and conduct follow-up assessments.

Workshops engage participants in a discussion about broader goals and purposes as well as an examination of whether their newsrooms' practices live up to those higher standards. They help an organization clarify its goals and develop strategies to achieve them. More than a dozen modules cover topics including Accuracy and Verification, Bias, Rethinking the News in an Online Age and the Meaning of Journalistic Independence. By 2006 the project had offered one-and-a-half-day sessions to more than 7,300 journalists in more than 120 print, broadcast and online newsrooms.

According to the CCJ, follow-up interviews, surveys and content analysis in newsrooms showed:

- An extremely high level of positive feeling regarding participation in the workshops.

- A strong and positive impact on participants' sense of purpose and morale regarding their journalism.

- Marked effects on the willingness and ability of participants to use critical thinking skills.

- Improvements in quality of the news product.

- Learning tools of good journalism, including verification, accuracy, investigative reporting, engaging and proportional storytelling and balance.

- Improved communication within the newsroom.

- Newsroom innovation dedicated to fostering better journalism practices.

For more information on the follow-up studies, go to www.concernedjournalists .org/node/547.

Stanford University professor William Damon and his research associate, Brett Mueller, shared data and other reporting from their follow-up assessments for *News, Improved.* The project has since moved to the University of Missouri with an additional $2 million grant from Knight. For more information, go to www .concernedjournalists.org/newsroom_development/traveling_curriculum.

## Tomorrow's Workforce

This $2.2 million project conducted assessments in 17 print newsrooms. (Partnerships also were offered to numerous broadcast outlets but none was willing to invest in training and publicly share any training successes.)

Tomorrow's Workforce (TW) conducted exhaustive assessments of newsroom training needs and identified practices and systems that might inhibit learning and the application of new skills. It followed up by helping newsrooms develop training that reflected newsroom goals and promised to improve communication and culture.

Of newsrooms where TW had conducted measurements and follow-up by the end of 2006:

- Five of seven showed overall progress in improving culture. Two others showed progress in the ranks of top and middle managers who had received intensive training and coaching.

- Eleven reported content improvements tied to training; those who decided to shift more focus online during the course of the project also linked progress to training.

The 17 assessed newsrooms—with more than 3,000 journalists—are:[1]

*The Atlanta Journal-Constitution* (daily circulation: 350,157)

*Columbus (Ga.) Ledger-Enquirer* (42,272)

*Dothan (Ala.) Eagle* (31,639)

*The Enterprise (Ala.) Ledger* (10,200)

*Gaston (N.C.) Gazette* (29,330)

*La Crosse (Wis.) Tribune* (31,941)

*The Modesto (Calif.) Bee* (79,638)

*The (Raleigh, N.C.) News & Observer* (165,483)

*The Oregonian* (310,803)

*Philadelphia Daily News* (112,540)

*The Philadelphia Inquirer* (330,622)

*St. Petersburg Times* (288,676)

*South Florida Sun-Sentinel* (222,183)

*Star Tribune (Minn.)* (358,887)

*Tri-City (Wash.) Herald* (40,927)

*Waco Tribune-Herald* (38,056)

*Winona (Minn.) Daily News* (11,192)

TW Director Michele McLellan and Associate Director Tim Porter are coauthors of *News, Improved*. In addition, management consultant Judy Pace Christie worked extensively with TW partner newsrooms.

## The Frontline Editors Project

As long ago as 1995 the news industry identified a crisis in the ranks of frontline assigning editors—the overtasked and often undertrained professionals who work

[1]Circulation figures from Audit Bureau of Circulation (ABC) or individual newspapers.

most closely with the news and staff. Pressures on those editors have snowballed with the expansion of the Internet and the shrinking of newsrooms. Despite the importance of those roles, leaders across the industry agree that assigning editors are among the least understood and least supported of all newsroom groups.

This project takes steps to close that gap, and hopes to encourage more training and support for frontline editors. A loose coalition of journalists, educators and news corporate representatives came together to find ways to boost understanding of the demands of the job in a changing media landscape, to identify and provide training opportunities to the editors in those positions and to help future editors step into those roles armed to succeed.

The project was funded with $100,000 from the Knight Foundation, Tomorrow's Workforce and Poynter's NewsU. Project partners worked with more than 100 educators and journalists, including 60 frontline editors, to create an inventory of noncraft skills required to be effective in the job. Job profile expert Les Krieger of the Assessment Technologies Group assisted in the project. The effort identified 23 key management, leadership and relationship skills for editors.

Working with Michele McLellan, director of Tomorrow's Workforce, and Jacqui Banaszynski, Knight Chair in Editing at the University of Missouri, NewsU now is using those findings to develop a wide array of online training for frontline editors. The first courses will be available in 2007, and include:

- A job fit assessment that will allow individual editors or prospective editors to compare their management style preferences with those of effective frontline editors.

- A module of newsroom situations, with optional responses, that will help those editors better understand their own management style on the job, and will provide feedback and refer them to training resources to help strengthen their skills.

- A day-in-the-life simulation course that will put prospective assigning editors into the job, helping them understand the challenges they might face and the skills they will need to be effective.

In addition to McLellan and Banaszynski, significant contributors to the project include Howard Finberg, director of NewsU; John Greenman, a former newspaper editor and publisher who is now a journalism professor at the University of Georgia; Marty Claus, a former executive with Knight Ridder; Carl Sessions Stepp, professor of journalism at the University of Maryland; Mary Nesbitt, managing director of the Readership Institute and associate dean at Medill, Northwestern University; and Michael Roberts, deputy managing editor for staff development at the *Arizona Republic*.

## The Learning Newsroom at API

The Learning Newsroom, sponsored by the American Society of Newspaper Editors and the American Press Institute (API), received a grant of $1 million in 2003 to work with 10 print newsrooms.

Through an intensive one-year program of training and facilitation of committee work, the project sought to demonstrate how training could improve the culture of the newsroom, a key driver of innovating greater audience appeal.

The Learning Newsroom developed a five-part culture-change curriculum, consisting of:

- *Communication.* Efforts to make communication more honest, direct and meaningful for individual and team performance.

- *Business literacy.* A better understanding of the strategies of the newspaper and how the work of all departments—newsroom, advertising, marketing and circulation—contributes to the enterprise.

- *Innovation.* An overview of ways in which organizations are identifying opportunities and responding with new products.

- *Systems analysis.* Looking at current practices, and suggesting more effective ones.

- *Time management.* Exercises to help staff recognize time-consuming practices that may no longer be efficient or necessary and stop or modify them.

More than 900 journalists received training from Learning Newsroom representatives while logging hundreds of hours with other trainers. Of seven newsrooms surveyed by the end of 2006, six had shown improvements in culture. Each participating newsroom also listed dozens of innovations and improvements in news content as a result of the project.

Participating newsrooms were:[2]

*Asheville (N.C.) Citizen-Times* (51,704)

*The Bakersfield Californian* (60,975)

*Bloomington (Ind.) Herald-Times* (28,886)

*Corpus Christi (Tex.) Caller-Times* (51,743)

*The Hamilton (Ont.) Spectator* (103,072)

---

[2]Circulation figures from Audit Bureau of Circulation (ABC) or individual newspapers.

*Lincoln (Neb.) Journal-Star* (76,504)

*San Jose (Calif.) Mercury News* (228,880)

*The Sarasota (Fla.) Herald-Tribune* (96,260)

*The Tacoma (Wash.) News Tribune* (116,150)

*The (Nashua, N.H.) Telegraph* (25,468)

Director Vickey Williams and consultants Pierre Meyer and Toni Antonellis contributed their research and advice for *News, Improved.* For more information on the project visit www.learningnewsroom.org.

## APME NewsTrain

With $1 million from the Knight Foundation and support from the Associated Press Managing Editors (APME), NewsTrain took craft and management training to more than 3,000 journalists at 40 regional locations between 2004 and 2006.

NewsTrain offers practical advice and proven techniques designed to help frontline editors polish their editing and management skills and become more effective editors. The program features two workshop leaders—a management teacher and an editing coach—as well as trainers on freedom of information, credibility and ethics, and online news.

In follow-up interviews and surveys of participants, John Greenman of the University of Georgia found:

- 95 percent found the sessions useful.

- Strong interest—80 percent—in training related to online news content, particularly editing and presentation for the Web.

- Greater willingness to advocate for training. More than half had participated in some form of training since returning from NewsTrain. Nearly two-thirds were stronger advocates for training in their newsrooms.

Elaine Kramer is project coordinator for NewsTrain, which was founded by Lil Swanson, NewsTrain's first director, and Carol Nunnelley, APME projects director. For more information, go to www.newstrain.org.

## ACKNOWLEDGMENTS

First and foremost we thank our Tomorrow's Workforce colleague Judy Pace Christie. Judy accompanied us on our many cross-country excursions to the newspapers in the project, sharing (too many) rental cars, (not enough) after-work libations and (endless) bowls of hotel oatmeal. We joked more than once that Michele's cup is always half full and Tim's is always half empty. Just as true, Judy's cup is always brimming over. In addition to her relentless enthusiasm, Judy's valuable insights into newsrooms and the journalists who populate them helped make the project successful. Her extensive interview material was invaluable for this book.

We also thank Tomorrow's Workforce program coordinator Helen Hutten, who managed our data, fact-checked and proofed drafts and kept us on schedule no matter how hard we tried to veer off it.

We thank all the smart people who talked with us for the book. Particularly helpful were insights from Sandy Rowe of *The Oregonian*, Julia D. Wallace of *The Atlanta Journal-Constitution*, Dana Robbins of *The Record* (Waterloo, Ont. Region), Mike Jenner of *The Bakersfield Californian*, John Smalley of the *La Crosse Tribune*, Bob Zaltsberg of the *Bloomington Herald-Times*, Mary Nesbitt of the Readership Institute and Pierre Meyer of MDA Consulting Group.

We thank our editors, Eric Newton, Kate Finberg and Jacob Arnold, for their patience, persistence and steady hands on the narrative tiller when we wandered off course, as we occasionally did. We also appreciate the contributions of Talia Greenberg and Anne Stewart of CQ Press.

And we thank Eric Newton—again—for bringing us together on one of the most rewarding projects either of us has worked on as a journalist.

Michele McLellan
Tim Porter